THE HAVES AND THE HAVE NOTS

ISBN 0-13-049766-5

9 790130 497665

FINANCIAL TIMES

Prentice Hall

In an increasingly competitive world, it is quality
of thinking that gives an edge—an idea that opens new
doors, a technique that solves a problem, or an insight
that simply helps make sense of it all.

We work with leading authors in the various arenas
of business and finance to bring cutting-edge thinking
and best learning practice to a global market.

It is our goal to create world-class print publications
and electronic products that give readers
knowledge and understanding which can then be
applied, whether studying or at work.

To find out more about our business
products, you can visit us at www.ft-ph.com

Pearson
Education

THE HAVES AND THE HAVE NOTS

The Abuse of Power and Privilege in the Workplace ... and How to Control It

Harvey A. Hornstein

FINANCIAL TIMES
Prentice Hall

An Imprint of PEARSON EDUCATION
Upper Saddle River, NJ • New York • London • San Francisco • Toronto
Sydney • Tokyo • Singapore • Hong Kong • Cape Town
Madrid • Paris • Milan • Munich • Amsterdam
www.ft-ph.com

Library of Congress Cataloging-in-Publication Data

Hornstein, Harvey A.
  The haves and the have nots: the abuse of power and privilege in the workplace--and
how to control it / Harvey A. Hornstein.
    p. cm. -- (Financial Times Prentice Hall books)
  Includes index.
  ISBN 0-13-049766-5
  1. Leadership. 2. Leadership--Moral and ethical aspects. 3. Organizational behavior. 4.
Supervision of employees. I. Title. II. Series.

HD57.7.H678 2002
658.4'0714--dc21

                                                                          2002075262

Editorial/production supervision: Techne Group
Executive editor: Jim Boyd
Manufacturing buyer: Maura Zaldivar
Editorial assistant: Allyson Kloss
Cover design director: Jerry Votta
Art director: Gail Cocker-Bogusz
Marketing director: Bryan Gambrel
Full-service production manager: Anne R. Garcia

© 2003 Pearson Education, Inc.
Publishing as Financial Times Prentice Hall
Upper Saddle River, New Jersey 07458

Prentice Hall books are widely used by corporations and government agencies for training,
marketing, and resale.

For information regarding corporate and government bulk discounts please contact:
Corporate and Government Sales (800) 382-3419 or corpsales@pearsontechgroup.com

Company and product names mentioned herein are the
trademarks or registered trademarks of their respective owners.

Printed in the United States of America

10 9 8 7 6 5 4 3 2 1

ISBN 0-13-049766-5

Pearson Education LTD.
Pearson Education Australia PTY, Limited
Pearson Education Singapore, Pte. Ltd.
Pearson Education North Asia Ltd.
Pearson Education Canada, Ltd.
Pearson Educación de Mexico, S.A. de C.V.
Pearson Education—Japan
Pearson Education Malaysia, Pte. Ltd.

FINANCIAL TIMES PRENTICE HALL BOOKS

For more information, please go to www.ft-ph.com

Dr. Judith M. Bardwick
  Seeking the Calm in the Storm: Managing Chaos in Your Business Life

Thomas L. Barton, William G. Shenkir, and Paul L. Walker
  *Making Enterprise Risk Management Pay Off:
  How Leading Companies Implement Risk Management*

Michael Basch
  *CustomerCulture: How FedEx and Other Great Companies Put the
  Customer First Every Day*

J. Stewart Black and Hal B. Gregersen
  Leading Strategic Change: Breaking Through the Brain Barrier

Deirdre Breakenridge
  Cyberbranding: Brand Building in the Digital Economy

William C. Byham, Audrey B. Smith, and Matthew J. Paese
  *Grow Your Own Leaders: How to Identify, Develop, and Retain
  Leadership Talent*

Jonathan Cagan and Craig M. Vogel
  *Creating Breakthrough Products: Innovation from Product Planning
  to Program Approval*

Subir Chowdhury
  The Talent Era: Achieving a High Return on Talent

Sherry Cooper
  Ride the Wave: Taking Control in a Turbulent Financial Age

James W. Cortada
  *21st Century Business: Managing and Working
  in the New Digital Economy*

James W. Cortada
  *Making the Information Society: Experience, Consequences,
  and Possibilities*

Aswath Damodaran
  *The Dark Side of Valuation: Valuing Old Tech, New Tech,
  and New Economy Companies*

Henry A. Davis and William W. Sihler
  Financial Turnarounds: Preserving Enterprise Value

Sarv Devaraj and Rajiv Kohli
*The IT Payoff: Measuring the Business Value
of Information Technology Investments*

Nicholas D. Evans
*Business Agility: Strategies for Gaining Competitive Advantage
through Mobile Business Solutions*

Kenneth R. Ferris and Barbara S. Pécherot Petitt
Valuation: Avoiding the Winner's Curse

David Gladstone and Laura Gladstone
*Venture Capital Handbook: An Entrepreneur's Guide
to Raising Venture Capital, Revised and Updated*

David R. Henderson
The Joy of Freedom: An Economist's Odyssey

Harvey A. Hornstein
*The Haves and the Have Nots: The Abuse of Power and Privilege in the
Workplace...and How to Control It*

Philip Jenks and Stephen Eckett, Editors
*The Global-Investor Book of Investing Rules: Invaluable Advice
from 150 Master Investors*

Thomas Kern, Mary Cecelia Lacity, and Leslie P. Willcocks
*Netsourcing: Renting Business Applications and Services
Over a Network*

Al Lieberman, with Patricia Esgate
*The Entertainment Marketing Revolution: Bringing the Moguls, the
Media, and the Magic to the World*

Frederick C. Militello, Jr., and Michael D. Schwalberg
Leverage Competencies: What Financial Executives Need to Lead

D. Quinn Mills
*Buy, Lie, and Sell High: How Investors Lost Out on Enron and the
Internet Bubble*

Dale Neef
E-procurement: From Strategy to Implementation

John R. Nofsinger
*Investment Blunders (of the Rich and Famous)...And What You Can
Learn From Them*

John R. Nofsinger
Investment Madness: How Psychology Affects Your Investing...
And What to Do About It

Tom Osenton
Customer Share Marketing: How the World's Great Marketers Unlock
Profits from Customer Loyalty

Richard W. Paul and Linda Elder
Critical Thinking: Tools for Taking Charge of Your Professional
and Personal Life

Matthew Serbin Pittinsky, Editor
The Wired Tower: Perspectives on the Impact of the Internet
on Higher Education

W. Alan Randolph and Barry Z. Posner
Checkered Flag Projects: 10 Rules for Creating and Managing Projects
that Win, Second Edition

Stephen P. Robbins
The Truth About Managing People...And Nothing but the Truth

Fernando Robles, Françoise Simon, and Jerry Haar
Winning Strategies for the New Latin Markets

Jeff Saperstein and Daniel Rouach
Creating Regional Wealth in the Innovation Economy: Models,
Perspectives, and Best Practices

Eric G. Stephan and Wayne R. Pace
Powerful Leadership: How to Unleash the Potential in Others
and Simplify Your Own Life

Jonathan Wight
Saving Adam Smith: A Tale of Wealth, Transformation, and Virtue

Yoram J. Wind and Vijay Mahajan, with Robert Gunther
Convergence Marketing: Strategies for Reaching
the New Hybrid Consumer

I don't say he's a great man. Willy Loman never made a lot of money. His name was never in the paper. He's not the finest character that ever lived. But he's a human being, and a terrible thing is happening to him. So attention must be paid.

Arthur Miller
Death of a Salesman [1]

Only little people pay taxes.

Leona Helmsley [2]

[1] From DEATH OF A SALESMAN by Arthur Miller, copyright 1949, renewed © 1977 by Arthur Miller. Used by permission of Viking Penguin, a division of Penguin Putnam Inc.

[2] Fletcher, J. "For mansion owners, a little-noticed tax break." *Wall Street Journal* (December 5, 1997): B1.

CONTENTS

PREFACE

Citizens everywhere are concerned about how powerful, privileged members of some companies are providing themselves with preferential treatment to the detriment of other employees, their own firms, and society at-large. This book explains why these people engage in such obviously destructive behavior (because their organizations encourage the expression of a natural human impulse called *we*-boosting), how *we*-boosting produces misuse of the three **R**s of organizational life (**R**ewards, **R**espect, and **R**ecognition), and what the adverse consequences of these events are on productivity, profits, and community support for business organizations.

Real illustrations, rich with the names of familiar organizations and business leaders, are plentiful. Every chapter also contains examples of individuals and organizations that are doing it right, and two chapters, entirely devoted to remedy, summarize the practical steps that some organizations are already taking to curtail this costly misbehavior.

Critics might complain that this book's concern with bosses' *we*-boosting tendencies and their management of the three **R**s places too much emphasis on the role of human forces in business organizations. They might even point out that from time to time, the book's seven chapters contain examples that seemingly contradict its call for improved management of the three **R**s by praising some business leaders and organizations that eventually failed, and by criticizing others that eventually succeeded.

These critics are shortsighted. It's true that the healthy profits that a strong economy produces often overcome the adverse financial effects of internal organizational disease. Special, well-protected marketplace niches, a company's unique competencies, technological advances, and product innovations are all capable of producing profits for internally troubled organizations. But the rest of the story, missed by these critics, is that excellence is not forever. Competitors are on the prowl. Imitation and invention are steadily shortening the half-life of any business advantage.

No one can guarantee that companies ensure their financial success by suppressing *we*-boosting and properly managing the three **R**s of organization life. All other things being equal, however, companies that learn how to suppress *we*-boosting and manage the three **R**s build employees' organizational identity, and they can expect to expand their success because of the competitive advantage that comes from having a workforce that is engaged.

Curtailing bosses' *we*-boosting and improving their management of the three **R**s is a business necessity, not a politically correct social nicety. Happily, the fact is that organizations possess the power required to make these changes and build crucial ties of organizational identification. Sadly, it is also true that—despite all the cheery business-section headlines to the contrary—bosses have frequently pursued a path leading to employees' alienation rather than affiliation.

As costly as such misconduct is now, it will only become more so. The changing attitudes and values of the workforce, increasing dependency of businesses on information processing, shortening cycle times for introducing new products and work processes, and rapid obsolescence of products and processes because of competitors' progress are just the beginning of a long list of trends in business and society that place a premium on employee innovation and initiative, drastically increasing the price that companies will pay for hindering the organizational identification of their workforce.

Remedies exist, but not in the form of magic formulas containing 10 rules that must be followed by business leaders who want to be successful. This book contains many examples of organizations that are both successfully curtailing bosses' *we*-boosting and managing the three **R**s of organizational life. Some of these examples are a part of today's business headlines; others were a part of yesterday's. In selecting examples to share, my priority was to provide you with a wide array of correct applicable illustrations rather than a more limited number of contemporary ones. Find examples that are right for you and tailor them to suit your company's current needs.

For nearly three decades friends, students, colleagues, and clients have shaped my understanding of organizations and organization change by sharing their views and commenting on mine. There are some who deserve special thanks. In alphabetical order they are Russell Ackoff, Billie Alban, Richard Beckhard, Caryn Block, Barbara Bunker, Warner Burke, Morton Deutsch, Jay Galbraith, Richard Hackman, Jerry Harvey, Ed Lawler, Harry Levinson, Roger Myers, David Nadler, Debra Noumair, Tony Petrella, Noel Tichy, Vic Vroom, and Ruth Wageman. Jim Boyd also deserves special thanks. In addition to having faith in this project, his creativity often surged when mine was flagging.

My daughters, Erica, Alison, and Jessica (in ascending order of their ages) listened to my ideas, becoming more adept at criticizing them as they grew older. Hannah and Samuel, my grandchildren, neither listened nor criticized, but I love them anyway. My wife, Madeline Heilman, has always listened to my ideas patiently, criticized them professionally, and supported me lovingly. Of course, this book is dedicated to her.

INTRODUCTION

Two hours into the flight, after finishing all the chit-chat about where we were coming from and going to, my seatmate asked me about the book that I'd mentioned I was writing.

I began with a question, although I didn't expect him to answer it. The answer was the reason this book was written.

"Why have 75 years of scientific inquiry and approximately two centuries of modern management experience made so little difference in the behavior of so many bosses? After all, the tactics for improving employees' sense of unity with the companies for which they work are no secret. In fact, even if there were no evidence or experience, common sense would probably be a pretty good guide to boss behaviors that help and hinder the growth of employees' identification with employers. So why do bosses continue to behave in ways that erode these important ties? And what about remedy? Can companies do anything to curtail the costly consequences of this misbehavior?"

I paused in order to give my seatmate time to ponder the questions' implications. Then I began my answer.

"Don't blame it on bosses' innocence, ignorance, or incompetence," I said. "Bosses continue to misbehave because traditional organizational arrangements inadvertently unleash *we*-boosting, a natural human impulse that prompts one group of people, bosses in this case, to elevate its status at the expense of others. The good news is that organizations have means for inhibiting bosses' *we*-boosting. The bad news is that they had better begin using them, because current business trends are already causing the sizable costs of this affliction to grow even larger."

"Bosses' *we*-boosting," I explained, "touches a button in every employee, beginning a downward spiral that steadily erodes employees' organizational identification. The button that it touches regulates employees' division of the world into in-groups, in which they include themselves, and out-groups, into which they banish others. This instinct to divide has profound implications for the work behavior of employees."

"When organizations are shoved into the out-group by bosses' *we*-boosting, ties of allegiance are severed. Showing up for work is not accompanied by any sense of belonging. Motivation to advance the organization's goals weakens, diminishing employees' productivity, commitment, loyalty, initiative, and willingness to perform the work of a good organizational citizen that—while not easily monitored—contributes to every company's success. Eventually, society suffers, as a steadily growing cadre of alienated working people learns to regard business organizations as the enemy, controlled by self-serving, arrogant bosses who have no interest in the well being of employees or the communities in which they live."

I paused when a wave of my seatmate's hand let me know that he wanted to break in. He launched into an account of his experiences with a previous employer, an insurance company, where he felt "treated like a thing, not a person."

I nodded, sincerely feeling sympathy and understanding for what he had experienced.

"Their only concern," he said, "was *what have you done for us today?* Despite all their inspirational b.s. and hullabaloo, to them I was just another piece of equipment—a tool. Bosses were the only 'important people' in the organization. It was one set of rules for *them* and another for *us*. They had no respect for me, and there was no mutual commitment. And if you're not for *me*," he declared, "then don't expect any more than that in return."

I asked him how his situation turned out.

"I left that company, ... eventually joined a competitor, and haven't ever felt a moment's guilt. I never did that before or since. But I did it to them because they didn't count me in. So I just counted them out."

My seatmate's experiences with his former employer are precisely like the ones I've heard about from hundreds of other working people. Taken together, these stories demonstrate the power that employees' sense of identification with their employers has to advance business goals, if it is properly and carefully developed, or to thwart them if it is not.

I have collected these stories over the course of three decades spent as a consultant to organizations seeking change. As an executive coach and management educator, I have also collected stories from hundreds of other employees in several different countries and many organizations. And at the same time, for more than 30 years as a professor of psychology at Columbia University, I studied the dynamics of employees' organizational identification and its links to bosses' arrogant displays of *we*-boosting.

Working with dozens of doctoral candidates, I spent lots of time investigating the effects of bosses' *we*-boosting on employees' sense of organizational identification, the consequences for work performance of the bond between employee and employer, and the strategies that have been successfully used by organizations to deter bosses' *we*-boosting.

Whether companies harness the power that comes from employees' identification with their employers or squander it depends on their capacity to maintain an efficient organizational hierarchy while battling bosses' misuse of the three **R**s of organization life, **R**ewards (Chapter 2), **R**espect (Chapter 3), and **R**ecognition (Chapter 4), in order to satisfy their natural tendency toward *we*-boosting (Chapter 6). Real workplace stories illustrate the challenge of battling bosses' misbehavior and offer practical strategies for winning that battle (Chapters 5 and 7).

A perfect example of how greatly work behavior is affected by employees' sense of identification with their employers is provided by the testimony of Joan Hoffman[1], a 32-year-old employee in a Massachusetts-based high technology firm. She told me of a time when she was leaving the company after a long day's work.

> *No one was around. I was the last person in my particular part of the site. No one was ever going to know that I was the last to leave. It was raining. I mean raining! I was dying to get home. My coat was zippered and Velcro'd when I paused near the exit doors in order to put on my hat. It was then that I noticed that banks of lights were burning in several areas where they should have been off. It was across the shop, several glass partitions away, but there they were, plain as day. It's one of those things that's not a big deal, but is a big deal when you think about it— if you know what I mean. Somewhere, probably in the*

facility's lower whatever, a utility meter was happily tick-ing away the added costs.

Now, to complicate things, I only vaguely knew where the switches were supposed to be. Even with that little bit of confusion, what was required should only cause me a three- or four-minute detour. Trotting across the empty space might take 30 seconds at most. Locating the controls could take a couple of minutes. But turning them off and getting out of there wasn't going to require more than another 30 seconds. Of course, if my decision was to forget it, to go on to my warm, inviting home, leaving the lights burning and the meters running, who would know? And that would mean zero time and effort for me.

What to do?

For now, suspend your concern about the story's ending. What would you do? This is a moment when employees' identification with their employers teeters in the balance, when a typical employee is caught between two options: to willingly expend effort on the organization's behalf, when one could avoid doing so with complete impunity; or to simply turn one's back and walk away.

I've asked more than 200 working men and women to ponder this choice. Their responses are almost always the same. Using words such as *loyalty, commitment, dedication,* and *emotional attachment,* these people agree that any employee who identifies with an organization would expend extra effort to help, while one who is alienated, lacking such ties, would turn away. Of course, this insight does not apply merely to spur-of-the-moment decisions about light switches. Scientific evidence from scores of investigations conducted by researchers in many countries confirms my respondents' innate understanding of the role that employees' organizational identity plays in an organization's success. Such research reveals the effect of employee allegiance and alienation on a wide range of every-day work behavior, and provides a basis for this book's practical guidance about what companies need to do in order to build crucial bonds of employees' organizational identification.

Reflect for a moment on your own feelings of organizational identi-fication. To help you consider your allegiance to your company, here are

10 statements commonly used for this purpose.[2] After reading each statement, rate how well it characterizes your current work experience by picking one of three choices: award one point for any thought or feeling that is *rarely* yours; mark two points for a thought or feeling that is *occasionally* yours; enter three points beside a thought or feeling that is *frequently* yours.

Rating

_____   1. Any criticism of my organization feels like a personal insult.

_____   2. What others think about my organization interests me.

_____   3. When talking about my organization, I usually say *we* rather than *they*.

_____   4. My organization's successes are my successes.

_____   5. Praise of my organization feels like a personal compliment.

_____   6. I feel strong ties to my organization.

_____   7. My organization is important to me.

_____   8. I don't regret being an employee of my organization.

_____   9. My organization is an important part of my self-image.

_____   10. I'm glad to be a member of my organization.

_____   **Total**

Although no precise mathematical boundary exists to clearly separate those who identify with their organizations from those who are alienated from them, experience shows that if you have a score of 22 or more, your allegiance to your company is healthy and intact. A score of 17 or less indicates withering allegiance and growing alienation.

If Joan Hoffman had responded to these statements, her total would have been considerably less than 17.

Alone in the office on that rainy evening, Joan Hoffman turned her back and walked away, leaving the lights burning. Joan rarely experienced her organization's successes and failures as if they were her own. When discussing her organization, she usually referred to it as *they*, not *we*. If others thought poorly of Joan's company, it was not much of a bother for her. Praise of her employer was not interpreted as personal compliment, nor was criticism regarded as insult.

How about you? How do you feel about your employer's successes and failures? Do you refer to the company that you work for as *we* or *they*? What are your feelings when others level praise or criticism at your employer?

Employees whose responses to these 10 questions total more than 22 are not like Joan Hoffman. They are reporting a blending of their own and their organization's goals. Because this blending causes them to vicariously partake of their organization's successes and failures, they are governed by a psychological golden rule of organizations: *Harming you becomes difficult for me because the two of us are part of* we. The tie that binds, producing this powerful statement, is the employees' organizational identification.

Unfortunately, this tie is often destroyed by arrogant boss behavior that is stimulated by a basic human inclination to *we*-boosting. In order to build the ties that bind, to erect the psychological golden rule of organizations, and to harness the power of employees' organizational identification, organizations must choose strategies that we already know are capable of curtailing bosses' *we*-boosting tendencies.

Choosing this organizational path is more easily said than done. As the next chapter shows, although today's organizations have more at stake than ever before and the time remaining for them to make the right choices is clearly running out, arrogant bosses continue to send employees the same alienating messages.

[1]The names being used for respondents are fictitious. Gender, age, and approximate position in the organization are accurate, however.

[2]Adapted from D. Abrams, K. Ando, and S. Hinkle. "Psychological attachments to the group: Cross-cultural differences in organizational identification and subjective norms as predictors of workers' turnover intentions." *Personality and Social Psychology Bulletin* 24 (1998): 1027–1039. These questions were used by my research team in several investigations involving hundreds of working men and women.

1

MESSAGES FROM BOSSES TO EMPLOYEES: ARROGANCE AND ALIENATION IN ORGANIZATIONS

"Working here is truly an unbelievable experience. They treat you with respect, pay you well, and empower you. They use your ideas to solve problems. They encourage you to be yourself. I love going to work."

Employee of Southwest Airlines, the company ranked number one in *Fortune* magazine's 1998 list of the "100 Best Companies to Work for in America"

You'd think that organizations would work harder to earn their workers' devotion and allegiance; after all, no psychological force helps in the achievement of organizational goals more than employees' identification with the companies for which they work. Employee initiative, risk-taking, and expressions of creativity—as well as increases in pro-organizational effort and decreases in counter-productive, self-serving work behavior—can all be linked to the presence of employees' organizational identification and can result in a more powerful company. Cross-cultural evidence from nations as widely separated as the UK and Japan shows that employee turnover is markedly diminished when identification with the company is strong, resulting in a major financial benefit to organizations.[1] A survey conducted by the American Management Association reveals that more than 50 percent of the organizations responding identified loss of talent as a primary cause of the decline in their companies' ability to compete in the marketplace.[2]

Workers' commitment to remain on the job translates directly into cash for the employer. In a study of 400 small- and medium-sized companies of whom 85 percent said "retaining key personnel" was a top concern, it was reported that the cost for replacing each senior manager was an estimated $50,000. Replacing an experienced worker cost these companies approximately $6,000, and the cost of hiring each new entry-level employee amounted to about $1,500. Whether your company's costs are more or less than these doesn't matter. Simply put, the point is that greater employee commitment means lower rates of turnover, and lower turnover means more profit.[3]

Financial consequences of personnel retention were also revealed in a recent study conducted by Ernst & Young. Analyzing the responses of 275 portfolio managers revealed that nonfinancial matters guided 35 percent of their investment decisions, and that one of the leading influences on these decisions was a company's ability to recruit and retain employees. Additional, anecdotal evidence that demonstrates the effect of good work-place practices on stock prices comes from the reports of financial analysts who acknowledge including the presence of "engaged employees" in their evaluation of companies.[4]

Even more direct evidence of the costs borne by companies populated with disengaged employees comes from a Gallup Organization poll. Finding that nearly one in five workers qualifies as disengaged, leads to the conclusion that "actively disengaged workers, based on their num-bers, salaries, and productivity cost anywhere from $292 billion to $355 billion a year."[5] These data leave little doubt about how much company worth is dependent on loyalty and contributory efforts that are contingent upon the employees' organizational identification.

The degree to which companies' worth is dependent upon employees' organizational identification has also become increasingly clear during the last two decades as key determinants of corporate success have migrated away from the realm of tangible assets and technology toward a harder-to-track ability to leverage employees' knowledge and information.

Baruch Lev and Paul Zarown's 20-year study of 6,800 companies shows that the relationship among financial statements, stock dividends, and stock prices is weakening. This means that during this period, variables in the companies' financial statements were increasingly less useful predictors of either future stock dividends or prices.[6] A principle reason for this decline is that traditional accounting information does not accurately index either the value of intellectual capital or organizations' abilities to make use of that capital in innovative ways. These findings are proof that while it would be foolish to argue that any accurate measure of a company's worth can completely neglect tangible assets and technology, it would be equally foolish to overlook the fact that a growing proportion of any company's value rests on its ability to harness employees' creativity, initiative, and commitment—all products of employees' organizational identity.

Further support for this conclusion comes from two professors of business, Theresa Welbourne of Cornell University and Alice Owens of Vanderbilt, who studied conditions associated with the survival of 136 companies in different businesses located throughout the United States. Only 81, or 61 percent, were still operating in 1993, five years after first opening their doors. Personnel policy made the big difference: 91 percent of those with both pay incentives (e.g., stock options or profit sharing) and some marker of general regard for workers, such as training programs, were around to celebrate their fifth anniversary. Only 34 percent of companies lacking these attributes survived that long. Seasoned investment strategists agree with the study's implications. Mary Farrell, a PaineWebber vice president and *Rukeyser Wall Street* television personality, has been quoted as saying, "In my checklist, there's a section on personnel issues," and many corporate observers and analysts are paying increased attention to those issues as well.[7]

The power of employees' organizational identification as a social adhesive with bottom-line consequences is also evident in *Fortune* magazine's annual report of the 100 best companies to work for in America. Comparing the average annual return to stockholders generated by firms that were nominated for the list by their employees with that of firms that were not, shows that investors were better off holding stock in companies that received employees' endorsements. Over a five-year period, these employee-approved companies returned 27.5 percent to investors, compared to only 17.3 percent among those not internally elected to the "Best 100." And over a 10-year period, those nominated returned 23.4 percent to investors, compared to only 14.8 percent among the unendorsed. This means that if an individual were persuaded to invest $1,000 in a firm boasting the emotional attachment of its employees, in eight years that money would have grown to $8,188. But if the same $1,000 were invested in a firm in which employees lacked such ties of allegiance, it would have grown to only $3,976 in the same amount of time.[8]

Organizational identification greatly influences companies' financial outcomes. In the words of a Gallup poll of 55,000 working men and women, corporate success is directly related to the presence of a workforce that can attest, "At work our opinions count; colleagues are committed to quality; we are given daily opportunity to do our best; and there is a perceivable connection between our work and the company's mission."[9]

Above and Beyond Job Descriptions

Organizational identification alters employees' personal job definitions. Those with stronger ties of identification define their jobs more broadly than those with weaker ones. As a result, they become more responsible, conscientious organizational citizens.

Successful organizational functioning depends on employees behaving like active citizens of the work community in ways that go beyond the narrow rigidities of formal job descriptions. In other words, companies *need* their employees to go "above and beyond." It's not surprising that one tactic employees use to hamstring their organizations during labor disputes is to narrowly conform to codified job requirements and insist on not making any effort beyond them.

Organizational citizenship behaviors (OCBs) imply extras.[10] Ambitious work habits are essential for organizational effectiveness, although they are almost never specified in job descriptions, nor normally included by name in performance evaluations. They are omitted because these "extra" work activities are difficult or impossible to monitor or quantify. Helping coworkers when one is not required to do so, being courteous (as opposed to simply not being *discourteous*), and going the extra yard when dealing with customers or vendors—not to mention turning off the lights when they are simply wasting money and energy—are just a few concrete examples of OCBs.

In my conversations with workers, I have discovered that some employees define their jobs as including OCBs while others see OCBs as merely add-ons, lying well outside their official job obligations and, therefore, unnecessary. Work, to the latter group, means doing only what is prescribed, monitored, and rewarded, no more, and less if you can get away with it. But to the former group, the jobs mean much more than that, and these workers, in turn, mean more to their companies.

The reason that some employees behave in ways that go "above and beyond" the bare minimum emerges from data collected by an organizational psychologist, Professor Elizabeth Morrison. Professor Morrison demonstrated that employees' emotional attachments to their organizations were associated with an expansion of their job descriptions.[11] What others saw as undesirable and irrelevant tasks, emotionally attached employees saw as duties that were essential and central to their job. Pro-organizational OCBs were a regular part of these workers' activities because they were perceived as right and necessary, even in the absence of organizational surveillance or sanction. The bonds of organizational identification between employees and their companies gave rise to job redefinitions that supported organizational goals, as well as to work, behavior that was a clear expression of the organizational golden rule:

> *Harming you becomes difficult for me because the two of us are part of we.*

When employees lack these bonds, on the other hand, damage to the company is likely to result. When workers feel that their interests and their organizations' are in clashing opposition, common sense and empirical evidence predict that self-serving work behavior is likely to result should employees find themselves in a position to do what's best for themselves without retribution. Without a counter-balancing sense of organizational identification, the most compelling choice among behaviors at work is the one that gains employees the most personal benefit at the least personal cost. If that choice also happens to help their organizations, then they might grudgingly assent. And if their selfish choice would harm their organizations, employees without emotional attachment are just as likely to go ahead with the action to the detriment of their employer.

Rates of in-company theft and sabotage—a high cost to companies around the world—are a vivid illustration of how employees behave in the absence of any sense of identification with their organizations. It comforts some to believe that these crimes are simply economically motivated efforts to make up for deficient wages, but the facts suggest otherwise. Workers at all income levels steal. What's commonly stolen tends to be petty and of little or no value to the thief. Sabotage, a common organizational crime, has no personal economic value for the employee-saboteur. And, most importantly, the evidence shows that employees tend not to steal from employers who treat them respectfully.[12] In short, workers more easily succumb to the temptation to rob or harm *them* rather than *us*.

Nonstop surveillance, backed by impressive reward and serious punishment, might be capable of deterring employees from making self-serving choices that go against organizational interests. But infallible surveillance is rarely possible and, even it were, worker compliance is a far cry from worker commitment. Behaving well before hidden cameras or curtailing one's anger for the sake of a bonus does not require any heartfelt blending of individual and organizational goals. Without such an internalization of the bond between worker and workplace, the golden rule of organizations—*Harming you becomes difficult for me because the two of us are part of* we—is not operative. The goals belong to *them*, not *us*, and employees' inclinations toward public compliance but private disobedience remain a potential hazard.

Happily, the fact is that organizations possess the power required to build crucial ties of organizational identification. Sadly, it is also true that—despite all the cheery business-section headlines to the contrary—bosses have mainly pursued a path leading to employees' alienation rather than affiliation. As costly as such misconduct is now, it will only become more so. Over the next several years, changes in business and society will serve to drastically increase the price that companies pay for hindering the organizational identification of their workforce.

Identification's Future

The intensity of the tides that have been tugging at organizations for a while is about to increase. According to a worldwide Anderson Consulting survey of 350 executives, an overwhelming 79 percent of those who were asked, "What will your company look like in 2010?" answered that the pressure to change will accelerate.[13] If they are correct, then adaptation is going to grow to unprecedented levels of importance as a competitive business tool. Successful adaptation surely requires having the right technology, information, finances, and market opportunity. But the key to adapting to market shifts is the presence of a workforce with the desire to contribute ideas about what *might be* and a willingness to let go of the familiar comfort of *what is*. Crucial to successful change are employees who will agree to and participate in major changes because their own goals and those of their organizations are more joined than separate.

Doing More with Less

Companies are increasingly required to do much more with fewer staff for a larger customer base than ever before. Periods of protection from competitors' responses to product innovations are shorter today than they were yesterday, and they will be shorter still tomorrow. Companies are able to copy rivals' products and processes with ever-increasing speed and ease. In response to the threat of such market incursions, companies are already seeking to shorten innovation cycles by organizing large sections of their workforces around temporary projects rather than permanent assignments. Personnel rosters not only are smaller, they are also constantly changing in composition so that managers can rearrange skill concentrations spontaneously and urgently. These onrushing events are aggravated by the mounting use of part-timers, of "virtual" workers (who are physically separate from work sites), and of temporary workers (currently some 30 percent of the workforce and, significantly, labeled *disposable* and *throwaway* workers by economists). The increasingly common use of nontraditional job arrangements widens the psychological distance between workers and employers, thereby worsening the prospects for success in future efforts to build the ties that bind employees to their organizations.

Leo Mullins, CEO of Delta Airlines, understood how a workforce's diminished organization identity undermines the potential power of technological innovation. When he became CEO during the summer months of 1997, the airline was a mess. Flight delays, lost luggage, fraying aircraft interiors, poorly served customers, and an angry staff were the carrier's hallmarks. Just a few years earlier, things had been very different. The airline was making money and it had a level of employee commitment that was envied throughout the industry.

Delta's problems began during the recession of the early 1990s. In order to deal with the economy's financial fallout, Ronald Allen, Delta's CEO at the time, probably paid too little heed to employee input and instead handed down his own measures designed to control and cut operating costs. Long before the program achieved its desired goals, however, it had to be terminated because of the devastating effects that it was having on employees' morale—and therefore on the service that they gave their customers. One Delta director, who was part of the effort to replace Mr. Allen with Mr. Mullins, explained why these adverse effects occurred. "You had a rending of the social contract that had existed for years and years within Delta."[14]

Leo Mullins' efforts, because they included rather than excluded the employees' needs and opinions, initiated a turning of the tide. In 1998, Delta earned a record-breaking $1 billion. There was a two-for-one stock split and a $50-million stock buy-back program. Lost luggage problems declined markedly and the airline's on-time arrival record pushed its ranking to number four among airlines, whereas it had previously been near the bottom of the heap. Part of Mullins' remedial effort focused on improving the company's computer systems, including innovations that gave Delta's gate agents more time to deal with customers. As Mullins pointed out, travel crises send airline customers rushing to the gate for help, and "that's where problem-solving expertise and expertise of the professional talent come in."[15]

Equipping employees with the best-tooled computer technology facilitates their expertise only if those employees choose to make that expertise available. Their willingness to contribute whatever knowledge they have acquired—on the spot, when not strictly supervised—depends on their psychological commitment to their employing organization and its goals. The need to develop this commitment within Delta's workforce was one of the main reasons why Leo Mullins spent so much time talking and meeting with Delta employees. Recognizing the costs of neglecting the labor side of the business equation, he explained his efforts by saying, "This is an organization where the trust factor suffered materially. I have been attempting as best I can to restore that, but it takes a long time because a lot of damage has been done."[16]

Going Global

Globalization serves to place an even greater premium on rapid adaptation as a competitive advantage. More and more pressure is being put on more and more companies to meet different and shifting customer demands of a suddenly worldwide scope. Maintaining sales volume and profits while matching product mix, quality, and other attributes to the idiosyncrasies of markets ranging from Brooklyn to Bangkok requires companies to be capable of mass customization—with unimpeded delivery—at the lowest possible prices. Lacking such abilities, companies will watch their customers, who are generally more loyal to self-interest and convenience than to any brand or supplier, flee to the nearest competitor.

Advances in computer technology undoubtedly increase the speed and ease of collecting and organizing information relevant to the challenges of globalization. But knowing what information to collect, whom and where to collect it from, and how to interpret the data's implications for product development and marketing strategies all require the expression of employees' insight and the exercise of their creativity. A readiness to make contributions such as these is characteristic of workers who are emotionally attached to their employers, not those who are disaffected and alienated from their jobs. Consequently, the rise or fall of companies competing in the global arena will be greatly affected by how well they manage to develop their workforce's organizational identification.

Globalization has also loosened the hold that corporate headquarters have on affiliates, granting them greater freedom—but often breaking the bond between employer and employees in the process. In expanding worldwide, many companies have abandoned landmark sites that they believe are too narrowly identified with one nation, a plan that backfires when it cuts off the feelings of identification that workers might have for such traditional sites. In 1995, for example, Pharmacia AB, a Swedish company, acquired Upjohn Cosmetics, a U.S. company based in Kalamazoo, Michigan.[17] The headquarters for the new company that resulted, Pharmacia Upjohn Inc., were placed in London, a location that decision-makers presumably hoped would prove more neutral ground. If so, it was a reasonable ambition, but the move might have ended up being no more than a costly eradication of a corporate symbol to which employees felt attached. Perhaps it is a good example of how bosses' *Field of Dreams* hopes that a new corporate identity and faithful customers will magically emerge once balanced arrangements and neutral sites have been constructed, are destined for disappointment, because they overlook the importance of workers' identification.

Outsourcing

Outsourcing, a growth industry these days, has also made company success more dependent on the thorough development of organization identity. Originally conceived as a cost-cutting tool, outsourcing is increasingly seen as a means for more effectively producing products and for serving internal and external customers. The idea is that by allotting certain tasks to firms outside the company, the firm can focus its personnel resources on a narrower range of tasks, and specialized skills and economies of scale will be developed in place of sprawling efforts to cover all bases.

Peter Drucker, an author and consultant with a half century of well-deserved fame for his insights about business and organizations, has predicted that within the next decade or two, all organizations' support work will be outsourced. He might be right, but before that happens, someone had better solve the problems that are afflicting outsourcing. A 1996 PA Consulting Company survey of companies in France, Germany, Denmark, Hong Kong, Australia, England, and the United States showed that one-third of the responding firms believed that outsourcing's disadvantages were greater than its advantages.[18]

Companies to which work and workers are outsourced face a different version of the common lack of emotional connection between employee and employer. Customers and clients, like some cousins, are "once removed." They are, in fact, part of *another* organization. This requires firms that receive outsourced work to build strong ties to their employees, so that their goal of serving someone else's employees and customers will become their own workers' goals as well.

Employing Generation X

During the next several years, certain existing social trends, if they continue, will add greatly to the difficulties of building ties of organizational identification. One example is the stylishly alienated behavior that's become a trademark of members of "Generation X." Converging evidence from a variety of surveys shows that young employees increasingly treat their employers' interests and their own as if they were incompatible. Their common resolution is to lean away from supporting organizational interests and toward satisfying goals that are more personal. From an individual perspective this might very well be an admirable activity; however, from a corporate perspective, it means that compensating measures are required—not necessarily to reverse the younger employees' personal decisions, but to offset the dysfunctional consequences to organizations. Successfully employing Generation X necessitates having policies of company management that create affiliation, not alienation, more effectively than ever before.

Investigators and observers are nearly unanimous in pointing out that the group of adults currently moving into the labor force in the United States and elsewhere in the industrialized world lacks a pro-organizational orientation. In a Coopers Lybrand study of 1,200 business students, 45 percent identified a "rewarding life outside work" as one of their lives' leading priorities.[19] And 68 percent of nearly 1,800 MBA students at major U.S. universities agreed "the family will always be more important to me than career."[20] In 1995, three-fourths of the respondents to a poll conducted by Penn, Schoen, and Berland supported the idea of giving workers a choice between overtime pay and compensatory time away from the job. They opted for the choice because, in their list of priorities, time often comes ahead of money.[21] The effect of this trend is as evident in the professions as it is in corporate business. For example, a *Law Practice Management Journal* article, titled "The Loyalty Crisis," complained about how young lawyers have less commitment and willingness to work the hours typically expected by law firms, preferring instead to focus on personal matters away from the office.[22]

There is reason to be uneasy about the wisdom and accuracy of branding an entire generation of human beings as being any one way. Generations do tend to share common experiences during their formative years, growing up with *Howdy Doody*, *Star Wars*, or the war in Vietnam, and a unifying batch of TV sitcoms and news programs offering a fairly homogeneous portrayal of world politics and events. But individual members of any generation also have experiences that are unique and idiosyncratic. In suburbia's country clubs, in urban tenements, and in rural malls, people have a diverse array of encounters that effectively distinguish them from the pack. Nonetheless, it is clear that employing organizations face a distinct uphill battle in seeking to earn the allegiance of the young people now at the beginning of their vocational lives. Generation X represents an additional challenge in the new obstacle course of employer-employee relations, joining globalization and outsourcing as changes in business conditions to which competitive organizations must swiftly adapt.

Managing *Us* versus Managing *Them*

Mentally dividing others into in-groups and out-groups clearly creates a psychological basis for the arousal of powerful emotions and motives, but scientists still wonder about the origins of human beings' readiness to separate others into categories of *Us* and *Them*.

Some say that its beginnings lie in animal evolution, wherein an ability to separate others into categories of *Us* and *Them* benefits its owners by seeding both intragroup cooperation and intergroup competition. Others argue that its roots can be found in early childhood experiences, wherein the development of an individual's self-esteem might be influenced by the act of judging the attributes of one's own family group against those of other groups. And a third contingent contends that the origins of the *Us versus Them* inclination can be found in the feelings of reinforcement that are associated with in-group membership: the sense of safety, security, and prestige that comes with belonging produces a powerful preference for others who are either familiar or similar. Regardless of this important debate's outcome, the immediately relevant point is that work behavior is greatly affected by employees' readiness to cleave their work worlds into in-groups and out-groups. From an organization's perspective, the most critical questions to ask are "Where does this division occur?" and "Why?"

If the organization is situated on the in-group side of its workers' mental division, then those employees experience a sense of identification with their employer, clearly revealed by their common reference to the organization in terms of *we*. However, should such a division place the organization on the far side of the boundary—away from self, on the out-group side—then its employees tend to speak of the organization as *they* rather than *we*. When companies are relegated to *they*, there is no feeling of worker-employer oneness, no merging of personal and organizational goals, and no vicarious experience of organizations' ups and downs. And when it comes to making decisions at work, self-interest—instead of the psychological golden rule of organizations—is the most accurate predictor of employees' behavior.

The good news is that companies can influence the boundary's location. In the abstract, the formula for successfully positioning the organization and its employees on the same side of the psychological dividing line is simple. It is a rule of reciprocity that says you get what you give: The beneficiaries of inclusion are inclined to include in return, whereas the victims of exclusion are inclined to exclude in return.

In recent years, many organizations have become aware of the danger of alienating their workers by making them victims of exclusion and have taken loud and well-publicized steps to prevent it. Such innovations as MBOs, SBUs, TQMs, T-Groups, and Theories X, Y, and Z, as well as catchwords like *brainstorming*, *delegation*, *process re-engineering*, *one-minute managing*, *Kanban*, *organization development*, *empowerment*, *participation*, and *culture change* create the sense that modern companies are hornets' nests of progressive and inclusive activity; but the truth is quite different. Deep and genuine change is still slow to come to organizations, despite the common misconception that such inclusion-inducing management practices are by now widespread.

The data concerning organizations' efforts to earn the allegiance of their workers is not encouraging. Recently, the U.S. Labor Department estimated that only 4 percent of U.S. businesses are involved in inclusion-inducing activities, such as genuinely empowering employees or developing a high-performance workplace.[23] Professor Edward Lawler, from the business school of the University of Southern California, reports that in a survey of the companies comprising *Fortune* magazine's *Fortune 1000* that was conducted by the University's Center for Effective Organizations, 68 percent of the firms claimed they used self-managed teams. However, any euphoria aroused by this apparently high percentage must be subdued by additional evidence showing that such teams included a mere 10 percent of the companies' workers.[24]

The reason for such a discrepancy between the reported popularity of inclusion-inducing approaches and their actual dissemination among companies and employees can be found in the results of a study by Boston-based consulting group Rath and Strong. In this research, 80 percent of the managers surveyed asserted that employees should have a voice in facilitating corporate change; yet when asked about *their own* employees, 40 percent of the same managers said they did not believe that the people who worked for them had anything valuable to contribute. Based on the judgments of these bosses about their subordinates, we can imagine how many fewer than 80 percent of them really ask for their subordinates' input when, instead of responding to a survey's questions about hypothetical conditions, they are actually on the job with the power to allow or disallow subordinate input.

Surveys of employees' views about their influence and involvement at work also support the conclusion that organizations' public pronouncements boasting of their inclusion-inducing approaches have exaggerated the frequency and effectiveness of such practices. In 1997, an annual survey of 3,300 employees conducted by Towers Perrin showed an alarming increase in both employees' feelings of disenfranchisement and the number of workers—approximately one-third—who claimed that their bosses ignored their interests when making decisions.[25] Similar findings come from a nationwide poll done by Princeton Research Associates in which nearly two-thirds of U.S. workers reported that their superiors could not be trusted to keep their promises.[26] Even at more senior levels, workers' feelings of personal influence and involvement appear to be eroding. For example, a survey of 196 executives of "40-something" age found that more than half of these senior-ranking workers felt less committed to their employers than they had five years earlier.[27]

The error of overestimating the presence of inclusion-inducing company practices is compounded by a second error: the myth that the executives in charge are regular and sincere users of these tactics. Even in the rare instances where such inclusive approaches have permeated employees' ranks, the programs' value is often nullified by the ulterior motives of their implementers. In companies these days, there is a lot of *faux* fellowship. Organizations' bosses try to appear caring in order to disguise a set of ulterior motives. Michael Hammer—a pioneer, along with James Champy, of the concept of "re-engineering" as a strategy for corporate change—acknowledged the pervasiveness of such fraud when he said: "The biggest lie told by most corporations, and they tell it proudly, is that 'people are our most important assets.' Total fabrication. They treat people like raw material."[28]

In-group members' vicarious experience of each other's plight serves to inhibit exploitative behavior in their dealings with one another. That is the golden rule of organizations' core message. On the other hand, a lack of such mutual allegiance inspires the opposite behavior. When employees conclude that bosses are treating them exploitatively, they feel excluded and exclude in return, shoving the organization icon away from themselves, deeper into out-group territory. The resulting separation squelches the development of employees' organizational identity, and opens up the possibility of treating the company the way its representatives treated them: as raw material, "things" to be exploited. It is the beginning of a downward spiral in which each exclusionary act by one group is paid back in kind by the other group, effectively separating the two further and further.

We would all like to be invited to be included, but we are not invariably blinded by that desire. When invitations are fraudulent, we quickly understand where to place our in-group/out-group boundary. Few of us are repeatedly duped when bosses unfurl the banner of inclusion and say, "Let's march together," only to show, through their later behavior, that they were silently adding, "Just keep your place—10 paces behind." Those in charge lose all credibility when, having declared "We're all in this together," they proceed—without prior warning and despite denials to the contrary—to dismiss 10, 20, or 30 percent of their workforce while granting themselves options with repricing privileges, special gross-ups, health plans with exclusive perks, and salaries plus bonuses that are more than 200 times greater than the average income of their employees. Yet it is important to recognize, however ironically, that these self-serving and duplicitous employers are actually demonstrating their keen understanding of a crucial cause of employees' organizational identity: that employers' motives affect the success of inclusion-inducing approaches. Their hope is that by pretending that their primary motive is attention to workers, they will fool employees into feeling included, embracing the organizations' goals as their own, and striving to achieve them.

Beyond this group of self-serving glad-handers is another batch of corporate authorities who dispense with the *all-for-one* pretense altogether. These bosses simply order the use of inclusion-inducing management technology regardless of the response by employees to the obvious lack of caring that accompanies it. Installed by dictate, company innovations that might actually have successfully unified bosses and workers not only fail to build such ties, but frequently break them. This is the third error made by those who believe that organizations are making extensive use of inclusion-inducing approaches: They overlook the crucial link between the *content* of these approaches and the *process* of their introduction into the workplace. Any sensible assessment of the impact of these innovations on organizations must begin by asking *how* their installation occurred, not simply whether they've appeared.

The manner in which new management methods are introduced determines their significance to the workforce. "You *will* be democratic" is a mildly funny joke, as audiences instantly recognize the inconsistency of the dictatorial command and the stated aim. Less funny, if similar, are organizations that introduce inclusive work programs in exclusionary ways—for example, through autocratic mandate—thus making employees pawns rather than participants in the process of change. What is unfortunately forgotten is that the programs' effectiveness rests on the *how* as well as the *what.* There is no top-down decision, however potentially beneficial, that cannot be undermined by uncommitted employees.

Mistaking *What* for *How*

Bosses who focus exclusively on the *what* of organizational change efforts, forgetting the *how,* are acting as if their employees are totally lazy and instrumental, caring solely about gains and costs, and seeking only ways of realizing the greatest personal financial gain with the least possible effort. Looking at their workforces through this lens, such bosses can easily conclude that improved job performance will be the product of a simple formula:

- *Prescribe* the tasks that authorities have decided must be performed in order to reach desired company goals.
- *Prepare* workers to perform those tasks.
- *Police* their behavior while they are performing them.
- *Pay* them for successful compliance.
- *Punish* them for failure.

If employees are as lazy and instrumental as these bosses presume, then this straight-and-narrow, command-and-control, carrot-and-stick calculus should work well. In fact, it turns out to be a dark and self-fulfilling prophecy. Predominant focus on the *what* by bosses produces alienation among workers, prompting their apathy and antagonism. Witnessing this attitude, then, only reinforces the initial convictions of bosses, who reason that it's precisely such deficient work behavior that makes necessary such an iron grip on their employees' productivity. "Unlike *us*," they think, "all *they* really care about is getting the biggest reward for the least effort." And increasingly—as workers are made to care less and less about an uncaring company—it becomes true. The result, in the minds of both management and workers, is a boundary that divides the in-group of elite bosses from an out-group of lowly employees.

Evidence against the merits of this autocratic ideology comes from both historical and current scientific examples. Nearly a century ago, Frederick Taylor's carrot-and-stick, time-and-motion efforts reinforced management's tendency toward this approach when his methods increased both worker productivity and, as wages were linked to output, workers' wages as well. Yet despite this tangible benefit, workers' discontentment with time and motion approaches grew.

Guided by an engineering model, time and motion efforts reduced tasks into their component parts, permitting "experts" to prescribe the most efficient *motions* for workers to use, in a given period of *time*, in order to get a job done. On paper, the prescriptions promised improvements in efficiency. But humans are a pesky lot. In practice, there is often a costly psychological backlash stemming from workers' feelings of being controlled.

In fact, things became so bad at one point that Taylor was called to testify before a committee of the United States Senate about his methods and workers' responses to them.[29] The employees' pain that offset Taylorism's gain was caused by workers' acute feeling of being *done to* rather than being *part of*. The case for workers' upset is undoubtedly puzzling to bosses who primarily focus on the *what* and disregard the *how*. There is evidently more to life than salary. No matter what the profits, if the rules of the game reduce workers to pawns, they will rankle employees as much today as they did a century ago.

In 1993, a *New York Times* headline alluded to a modern manifestation of that very rankling: "Strikers at American Airlines Say the Objective Is Respect." The article reported: "It is not so much the pay or benefits or sometimes grinding four- and five-city, one-day trips or the interminable, unpaid delays between some flights. It is the little things that striking flight attendants at American Airlines say grate on them and amount to a lack of respect. 'They treat us like we're disposable, a number,' said Helen Neuhoff, a 33-year-old flight attendant." Another attendant said: "I'd rather be on the planes. But I've got to stand up for what I believe. My self-respect is more important than my job."[30]

Nor did the issue go away. Four years later, when troubles at American Airlines brewed again, the theme remained the same. A disgruntled pilot complained, "As long as you treat your employees as merely 'unit costs,' like the Styrofoam coffee cups we throw out after every flight, morale will remain at rock bottom."[31]

Comments made by a disenchanted employee in the automobile industry capture the implication of these quotes—and serve to invalidate the all-too-common view that for employees, it's all about money.

> *We're a cost. That's it. In their [pointing upward] world we're not human beings who have thoughts, a life filled with ordinary joys and worries, feelings. Their focus is on the bottom line and to them we're simply lines on a budget that are labeled 'cost.' And they figure that about ninety-five percent of what gets me going in the morning is caring about how to get the most for the least—when, really, it's not even like one percent of what gets me going. What they believe, it's insulting.*

Boss behavior that is based on a decidedly *what*-oriented image of employees is entirely inconsistent with overwhelming evidence showing that *how* people are treated, rather than the benefits they receive, best predicts their willingness to support organizational goals.[32] A recent study involving 2,800 federal employees demonstrated that their views on the fairness of decision-making procedures were more than twice as powerful an indicator of their evaluations of management as their views about pay.[33] Rewards and punishments certainly affect employees' work, but bosses' fair and respectful treatment of them is by far the most powerful tool to earn their commitment.

Moving Toward *We*: The Three Rs of Work Life

In my many conversations with bosses who defend their *what*-orientation, I've been told that without strict adherence to the *Prescribe, Prepare, Police, Pay, and Punish* formula, the great majority of workers will not do their jobs. "Ask the average employee to join in a real problem-solving discussion at work," they say, "and the response is either belligerence or a blank stare." My response is: Did they begin that way? Did they arrive on day one of their new job completely devoid of any desire to innovate, initiate, achieve, or explore any creative ways of making their work environments more productive and satisfying? If not, then could the belligerent, blank response possibly be a consequence of receiving hundreds—perhaps thousands—of messages from bosses that effectively alienated them, erasing any sense of identification with their organizations and eroding their job commitment?

This is not to say that developing employees' organizational identification is a panacea for all workplace ills. It is a major contributor to an organization's success, but not its sole cause. In excess, the very same powerful in-group dynamics that encourage workers to advance their company's goals can in fact prove harmful. Narrow, intense allegiance to a firm has even been the basis for employees' criminal efforts to benefit their organization at the expense of others. The conditions that give rise to such overzealous and unconstrained obedience, as well as the steps that can be taken by organizations to avoid them, are discussed in this book's closing chapters. Nonetheless, these perils are rare in comparison to the great potential that arises from workers' sense of identifying with their employing organizations.

In every firm, company, and workplace, employees are watching for messages contained in their bosses' practices and policies in an effort to decide whether they are being viewed as *We* or *They.* Workers use these data, whether overseen or overheard, stated or implied, to answer certain core questions about their relationships to their jobs:

Do my bosses only care about the quality of the product I deliver, without any authentic regard for me as its producer?

Do my bosses have any genuine concern for my concerns, or am I regarded simply as a machine that must perform to or above the standards they have set?

Do my bosses view workers like me as interchangeable, or do they see me as an individual, not simply a number?

Am I merely hired, or am I truly a member of the firm?

Guy Wolff, an employee of an agri-business in the United States' Midwest, captured the essence of these questions when he told me, "They say *take the job personally*; then they go ahead and treat me impersonally." Hundreds of other workers have pointed angrily to the same paradox. The preceding important queries boil down to a single question, which concerns the three **R**s of life at work: **R**ewards, **R**espect, and **R**ecognition:

> *Am I treated fairly, with genuine civility, and with proper recognition of my abilities?*

Unfortunately, employees are regularly led by bosses' messages to answer a resounding "No." In every chapter that follows, practical examples—gleaned from organizations that have successfully grown ties that bind—offer precise prescriptions for bosses at every level to turn that answer to "Yes," and to change a previously alienated worker into an engaged, loyal, and powerful force capable of the achievement of organizational goals and personal satisfaction at once.

Any organization's success relies on employees' organizational identity; and identity is built on bosses' handling of **R**ewards, **R**espect, and **R**ecognition. The next three chapters tell the story of what's going wrong, and how the three Rs can be revived to the benefit of employer and employee alike.

---

[1] Abrams, D., K. Ando, and S. Hinkle. "Psychological attachments to the group: Cross-cultural differences in organization identification and subjective norms as predictors of workers' turnover intentions." *Personality and Social Psychology Bulletin* 24 (1998): 1027–1039.

[2] Fisher, A. B. "The 100 best companies to work for in America." *Fortune* (January 12, 1998): 69–70.

[3] Carey, P. M. "6 sweet ways to keep your key players." *Your company* (August/September, 1996): 44–47.

[4] Ibid.

[5] "Work Week." *Wall Street Journal* (March 13, 2001): A1.

[6] Stewart, T. A. "Real assets, unreal reporting." *Fortune* (June 6, 1998): 207–208.

[7] Hemlock, D. "I.P.O.'s: When employee-friendly = investor-friendly." *New York Times* (February 25, 1996): F4.

[8] Grant, L. "Happy workers, high returns." *Fortune* (January 12, 1998): 81.

[9] Ibid.

[10] In E. D. Morrison, "Role definitions and organization citizenship behavior: the importance of the employee's perspective." *Academy of Management Journal* 37 (1994): 1543–1567, the five areas of organization citizenship behavior have been defined as being Altruism (helping when it is needed but not required), Conscientiousness (going beyond what is minimally required), Civic virtue (being a responsible participant in the organization's life), Sportsmanship (tolerating the ordinary glitches without undue complaining or grieving), Courtesy (working and playing well with others).

[11] Ibid.

[12] Altheide, D. L., P. A. Adler, P. Adler, and D. A. Altheide. "The social meanings of employee theft." In *Crime at the Top: Deviance in Business and the Professions*, J. M. Johnson and J. D. Douglas (Eds.) (Philadelphia: J.B. Lippencott, 1978): 90–124.

[13] Moran, N. "Change is only the beginning." *The Daily Telegraph* (May 28, 1997): 3.

[14] Taylor, A. III. "Pulling Delta out of its dive." *Fortune* (December 7, 1998): 158.

[15] Ibid.

[16] Ibid.

[17] Markels, A. "Building a new house." *Wall Street Journal* (September 26, 1996): R23.

[18] Moran, N. "Look to corporate federations." *The Daily Telegraph* (May 28, 1997): 2.

[19] "Work Week" *Wall Street Journal* (June 3, 1997): A1.

[20] "What the new generation really wants." *Fortune* (April 14, 1997): 157.

[21] Alston, C. "Comp time's time has come." *Wall Street Journal* (May 15, 1997): A22.

[22] Zinober, J. W. "The loyalty crisis: Today's employee is quite a different breed from yesterday's." *Law Practice Management* 18 (April 1992): 26–32.

[23] Swaboda, F. "Conference tries to define 'High-performance' jobs." *Washington Post* (July 27, 1993): D1, D5.

[24] Dumaine, B. "The trouble with teams." *Fortune* (September 5, 1994): 86–92.

[25] Shellenbarger, S. "Investors seem attached to firms with happy employees." *Wall Street Journal* (March 19, 1997): B1.

[26] Repic, E. "Manager's casebook: Re-engineering and morale." *Engineering Management Journal: EMJ* VII (June, 1995): 4.

[27] Burkins, G. "Work Week." *Wall Street Journal* (May 20, 1997): A1.

[28] Lancaster, H. "Re-engineering authors consider re-engineering." *Wall Street Journal* (January 17, 1995): B1.

[29] Kanigel, R. *The One Best Way* (New York: Viking, 1997).

[30] Kilborn, P. T. "Strikers at American Airlines say the objective is respect." *New York Times* (November 22, 1993): A1, A8.

[31] Gwynne, S. C. "Flying into trouble." *Time* (February 24, 1997): 46–49.

32 Tyler, T. "The psychology of legitimacy: A relational perspective on voluntary deference to authorities." *Personality and Social Psychology Review* 1 (1997): 323–345.

33 Tyler, T. R. and E. A. Lind. "A relational model of authority in groups." In *Advances in Experimental Social Psychology*, ed. M. Zanna (New York: Academic Press, 1992) 25:115–191.

2

THE FIRST R—REWARDS:
COMPENSATING
PRIVILEGE

In June 1998, a fast-food industry employee was quoted as saying, "McDonald's isn't paying its middle managers any bonuses this year, but the CEO gets a bonus of $1 million.... And they wonder why they have trouble holding on to good employees."[1]

Two years earlier, the increase in the total pay package of IBM's CEO, Louis V. Gerstner Jr., over what he had received the previous year, was reported to be almost 30 percent, giving him an annual income of about $20.2 million. Admittedly, it was a terrific year for IBM. One index of the company's success, its stock's market value, rose approximately $43 billion. Consequently, in addition to rewarding Mr. Gerstner, the company decided to award its 241,00 employees with cash bonuses averaging 10 percent of their pay.

Two IBM employees with whom I spoke shrugged their shoulders when I asked them about the discrepancy between their 10 percent and Mr. Gerstner's 30 percent. With obvious resignation, one of them complained, "If he, and those at his level, had given up a bit, we could have gotten a bit, or maybe we all just could have gotten the same percent, and that would have been more reasonable." With evident sarcasm, the other suggested, "Maybe they really needed the additional millions."

Fast forwarding two years, returning to 1998, when Mr. Gerstner's remuneration gain was again disproportionately greater than that of the average IBM worker, an employee of the company was recorded as saying, "Sure, Lou Gerstner has done a terrific job here, but he hasn't done it alone.... but while he gets $2 million in new options, the rest of us will settle for a 3 percent raise this year—if we're lucky."[2]

Mr. Gerstner's gains in salary are not unusual at his level.[3] In 1999, CEOs of 55 large companies that were surveyed by a management compensation firm earned 24 percent more than they did in 1998.[4] That increase in their income is several times greater than the growth of either other employees' compensation or corporate profits.[5] This trend continued a year later, in 2000, when CEO salaries averaged a 22 percent gain, while the value of the typical investor's stocks declined 12 percent, hourly workers averaged a 3 percent raise, and salaried workers averaged a raise of 4 percent.[6] And, in 2001, when a 35 percent decline in company profits was typical, median executive compensation still grew by 7 percent, twice the rate of increase enjoyed by the average worker.[7]

According to Graf Crystal, arguably the world's leading expert on executive compensation, two decades ago CEOs typically earned 40 times more than their firms' average worker. But at the onset of the third millennium, they are earning approximately 200 times more.[8]

More Than Money

Differences in pay have an effect on employees that goes beyond their pocketbooks. Consider what happened at Boeing on Tuesday, November 21, 1995. After being on strike for nearly 50 days, 30,000 Boeing Company machinists, members of the International Association of Machinists and Aerospace Workers, voted on an offer made by management that previously had been unanimously endorsed by their union's leadership. The offer provided Boeing's workforce with greater control over the displacement of jobs to foreign shores, reduction of health care premium costs, and a one-time 5 percent bonus based on their annual wages. (At the time, these workers averaged $22 per hour.)

Tabulation of the ballots showed that more than 60 percent of the strikers voted "No!" For the first time in the union's history, workers had disregarded their leaders' recommendation. Analysts claimed that one obstacle to a "Yes" vote was an antagonizing disparity in the rules for distributing rewards between bosses and employees. On that Tuesday, the day of the vote, the closing stock price on Boeing shares crossed a threshold, making individual Boeing executives eligible for special bonuses amounting to as much as $5 million.

Boeing had done well. Share prices had risen over 75 percent during the previous two years. Profits in the preceding year, 1994, had reached $800 million. Reportedly, workers did not object to executives receiving special incentive bonuses—it was the magnitude of the asymmetric distribution between their share of the pie and executives' share that bothered them most. How much it bothered them was captured in the words of one employee with a 22-year history at Boeing: "All along, we've been told that we're world-class workers, part of the team that is the world's leading airplane maker.... I worked my tail off helping the company get through its rough times. They ought to spread the appreciation around."[9]

Failure to share appreciation with everyone who contributes to a company's success evidently contributed to United Parcel Service's (UPS) costly labor unrest in 1997.[10] According to James Champy, co-author of *Re-engineering the Corporation*, despite outward appearances, "In reality ... the UPS has historically suffered from mismanagement; one that has ignored its customers' needs and *misunderstood the important role employees play in its profits*."[11]

Between 1992 and 1996, UPS reportedly doubled its profits, finally reaching $1.15 billion. Despite the firm's success, UPS drivers' pay, adjusted for inflation, had not risen in nearly 10 years. Adding aggravation to these acts of managerial neglect was the company's practice of paying permanent employees $20 an hour, while giving part-timers (equaling about 60 percent of the workforce at that time) only $11 an hour for the same work.

During this same period, despite a record number of injuries, UPS also raised the weight limits of packages that drivers had to lift. In response, an expert at Cornell University's School of Industrial and Labor Relations said, "UPS has one of the worst health and safety records. The company has an injury rate that is two and a half times the industry standard."[12] This dismal record was undoubtedly one reason why UPS paid an estimated $4.4 million to settle employees' health and safety claims during the seven years preceding the labor unrest. Rather than being seen as a sign of caring that placated workers, these settlements might actually have increased worker alienation. They can be interpreted as containing a message from UPS management that says, "It's cheaper to let *them* get harmed and pay for it, than for *us* to change *our* profitable productivity requirements." That type of instrumental thinking clearly ranks profits above people, while simultaneously categorizing employees as members of an expendable out-group. In August 1997, about 185,000 UPS employees answered their management's unappreciative messages of exclusion by launching a lengthy, bitter, and occasionally violent strike.

Spreading appreciation around is something that Fleetwood Enterprises, located in Riverside, California, seems to have accomplished. Fleetwood's compensation scheme builds employees' cooperative attachment to one another and to the organization as a whole by using explicit compensation formulas, tailored to fit an employee's position, in order to link pay to performance. Throughout the organization, from top to bottom, base salaries are comparatively low, but incentive opportunities for supplementing that base are high[13]: Senior managers, for example, receive stock options annually and incentive bonuses twice yearly, *if* Fleetwood's return on invested capital equals or exceeds its cost of capital. Plant managers' stock options and bonuses, on the other hand, depend on their plants' profits, while production workers' bonuses depend on their plants' productivity. Other Fleetwood Enterprise rewards mesh well with this pay scheme, sending a clear message of inclusion to employees. Walk through this *perkless* company and you will find no executive dining rooms or special parking spaces. Fleetwood's chairperson flies coach to business meetings, and observers describe the company's senior executive offices as "ordinary."

Arranging rewards in this way has a profound affect on Fleetwood workers' sense of identity with the organization. As one of them said, "Senior management doesn't appear separate from the organization, but is a part of it," adding, "It builds trust...if the company does well, we all share in the rewards."[14]

Obviously, money does more than affect employees' pocketbooks. When rewards are properly structured, they say to employees, "We are in this together, either sinking or swimming as a unit. No one here has special access to life jackets." For employees, this message of inclusion tends to produce inclusion in return, encouraging them to move their mental image of the organization to a location on the in-group side of the in-group/out-group boundary, where it becomes part of *we*. With this developing sense of organizational identity, organization and individual goals merge, giving birth to the psychological golden rule of organizations: *Harming you becomes difficult for me because the two of us are part of* we.

When discrepancies in rewards, and in the organizational procedures used by organizations to determine those rewards, exceed what employees regard as either rational or appropriate, they break ties between employees and employers, build we/they boundaries, and diminish the workforce's organizational identification. Instead of sending messages of inclusion, bosses who feather their nests send arrogantly-toned messages of exclusion, a bit like the one that follows:

> *"The differences between us do not and need not con-form to any rule of justice or fairness. We are not obliged to use some common denominator in calculating your compensation and ours. The yardstick that we use for computing your compensation may employ precisely defined indices of ability, effort, or entrepreneurial risk that have no bearing on how we compute our compensa-tion. We are a part of a class of people who have the power to give you rewards using rules from which we may choose to exempt ourselves. We will pay you what those rules require and pay ourselves according to the customs of compensation that are applicable to people like us."*

Compensating Privilege

Imagine, or, if you have had the experience, recollect what it was like to lose your job and learn afterward that senior executives' incomes increased 28 percent over levels that existed in the previous year, to an average of $4.1 million. That is what happened to many U.S. workers in 1993, a year in which existing records for layoffs were broken.[15]

Next, imagine, or, if you have had the experience, recollect what it was like to receive an annual raise of $900 (3 percent of $30,000) or even $3,000 (3 percent of $100,000). Then you learned that senior executives were averaging double-digit raises of 20 or even 30, 40, or 50 percent. That was the experience of most U.S. wage earners in 1996. It was a year in which individual salaries actually averaged less than $30,000, the year-to-year salary increase over 1995 for the average wage earner was approximately 3 percent, and only a small percentage of the workforce enjoyed annual incomes of $100,000.

Continue your mental journey by pretending that another year has passed. It is now 1997, a year in which you, *the average worker*, saw your total wages and benefits increase 3.1 percent, while senior corporate exec-utives' average increase was 29 percent, growing the median level of their total compensation to $3,093,018.[16] Now leap ahead two more years, to

1999. You are a nonunion salaried worker. Your income increase over the previous year was 4.2 percent, which puts you exactly at the midpoint of increases received by nonsalaried workers. But while reading your local newspaper, you learn that the 1999 year-to-year increase of salaries and bonuses for CEOs standing at the midpoint of their group was 11 percent, more than two and one-half times greater than your increase.[17]

One year later—it's 2000 now—you read the same newspaper. Things have changed: Although the average raises for hourly and salaried workers are only 3 and 4 percent, respectively, this year CEOs' salaries and bonuses grew by a whopping 22 percent. Is this change attributable to the CEOs' superlative performance? Not likely: The annual profits for the Standard and Poor 500 companies grew at less than one-half the rate they did through the 1990s.[18] Stockholders everywhere were suffering serious financial loss.

Bosses who give themselves access to rewards they deny to other employees create discrepancies that contribute to crushing employees' organizational identification. Large portions of their compensation are composed of guaranteed payments that transport them, and them alone, into privileged, protected, financial preserves where they are insulated from any adverse consequences of either their performance or the organization's.

Option grants, quite possibly the single greatest reason for the disproportionate rise in executive compensation, are a primary tool (*mis*)used by bosses to provide themselves with protection by unhinging their pay from performance. Labeled "stealth compensation" by U.S. Senator Carl Levin,[19] options are remuneration beyond salary and bonus. They provide the receiver with rights to purchase shares of company stock at a set price—called the *strike price*—during a predetermined period of time.

According to a survey released in January 2000, more than 80 percent of the workforce is denied opportunity to receive option grants.[20] Even among the remaining 20 percent, some are more eligible than others are. Commonly, an option grant's availability is restricted to an exclusive senior management group, with almost one-third of all options going to organizations' top five executives.[21] Moreover, for this small group, during the past several years, option grants have become an increasingly large part of total compensation. Between 1992 and 1997, for example, a period during which senior executive compensation is estimated to have doubled, more than one-half the increase came from option grants.[22] In some years, for CEOs, option grants have been as much as five times greater than salary.[23] By 1999, the average grants given to CEOs and senior management were valued at $3.2 million and $681,000, respectively. In 2000, a study showed that "the value of options granted at the 325 largest companies in the United States equaled almost 20 percent of their pretax profits," leading to the conclusion that a lot of money that might have gone to shareholders went to executives.[24] If some want to argue that executives deserve the compensation because of their contribution to earnings, then what happened in 2001 should trouble them. In that year, despite declining revenue and profit, the flow of options to executives continued unabated.[25] The renowned investor Warren Buffett strongly criticized this means of lavish salary supplementation, saying, "There is no question in my mind that mediocre CEOs are getting incredibly overpaid. And the way it's being done is through stock options."[26]

When option grants are properly employed, their use as rewards for employees has considerable merit. Because improved organization performance might lead to rising stock prices, options provide holders with incentive to work in ways that promote company success. If the stock's price exceeds the options' strike price during the specified time period, then the options can be exercised, giving the holder profits from the sale. If, however, the stock price during the options' lifetime remains below the strike price, then the holder might be forced to allow the options to lapse, without realizing any profit whatsoever. Thus, options have the potential to merge an organization's success with an individual employee's self-interest. Unfortunately, that potential cannot have wide influence on a workforce as long as options remain the disproportionate privilege of senior management, as they currently are. Further, a widespread abuse, called "repricing," has obliterated options' *pay-for-performance* contingency, thereby removing their incentive value even for the few who get them.

Repricing simply provides option holders with a new purchase price, usually lower than the original strike price. Consequently, even if their company's share price falls because of lackluster performance, which they might have caused, members of the elite repriced-option holders' club remain in a position to realize a profit. Repricing removes risks (a benefit possessed by no ordinary stockholder) and undermines incentive. For the elites, it is a heads *we* win, tails *we* win deal.

Does repricing happen? All the time, despite rulings by the Financial Accounting Standards Board attempting to discourage the practice.[27] According to the Investor Responsibility Research Center, more than 300 companies repriced options in 1999. Stanford University Business School Professor Charles O'Reilly reports that between fiscal years 1995 and 1998, Apple repriced options six times.[28] Stock prices of another company, Grand Casinos Inc., dropped to $26 per share from $35 per share in about

12 months. Halfway through that period, the company's board changed the price at which Grand Casinos' CEO Lyle Berman could buy shares, to $11 from $32. With that change, if Mr. Berman were then to sell his stock at $32 per share, the original strike price, he would allegedly have earned more than $20 million. Stockholders, who bought shares at $32 and sold along with Mr. Berman, would have earned a net profit of zero, if you disregard the interest they lost by not simply keeping their money in the bank.

Some companies avoid repricing, but guarantee profits, by giving option holders additional options when the price of their original holdings falls. Other firms simply reimburse option holders for options that have lost value, allowing them to make new purchases when the market is more favorable.[29]

For another variation on the repricing theme, let's go back to 1995, when business pages of magazines and newspapers applauded H. Wayne Huizenga for taking command of Republic Industries—a Ft. Lauderdale, Florida, holding company for an array of businesses—while refusing any salary and bonus for the year. A couple of years later, events at Republic won less applause when 750 of the organization's most senior bosses, including Mr. Huizenga, received options at a strike price set at a value the stock had reached several days before the options were granted, which happened to be the lowest in nearly three months. Knowledgeable commentators characterized this procedure as a departure from the conventional practice of setting options' strike prices using the company's stock price at the close of business on either the day that the grant is made or the previous day. According to reports, Mr. Huizenga's options gained $2.7 million. This type of deal probably makes it easy to forget about forgone salary. It is not a deal that is available to most employees.

Conduct a mental experiment contrasting the effect on ordinary employees of repricing executives' options with the effects that undoubtedly occurred because of how Mr. Lew Platt, former CEO of Hewlett-Packard, dealt with company stock that he was given. A large package of Hewlett-Packard stock that he received in 1996 was going to become his three years later *if*, by that time, the company's performance met a set of prespecified criteria. If, however, Hewlett-Packard's performance did not satisfy the criteria, Mr. Platt would forfeit the stock. This contingent benefit was an incentive to excel.

Measures taken after the three years had passed showed that the firm's performance had not successfully crossed the critical threshold. But neither repricing nor compensatory payments provided Mr. Platt with a special rescue. Despite his salary ($1.8 million) and options, Mr. Platt's total compensation for the year fell by 75 percent. He and his organization abided by the original promise. Mr. Platt returned the stock, which had an estimated value of $2.4 million.[30]

Exceeding the performance goals would certainly have been a better outcome for all involved. But if that was not to happen, for whatever reasons, then Mr. Platt and Hewlett-Packard at least avoided a double whammy by resisting the temptation to void the rules, send messages of exclusion to the workforce, and fray employees' ties of organizational identification.

Repricing (including Republic's innovative variation) unlinks pay and performance, destroying the motivational value of options. It removes the incentive for recipients to think like owners. They are going to win no matter how well or how poorly they play the game. Even without repricing, options are frequently without motivational benefit because their timeline practically guarantees a win. When an option grant provides holders with plenty of time to exercise their privilege (sometimes extending for as long as 10 years), it allows them to wait beyond their job tenure, through normal oscillations of the stock market, to a time when the stock's price is higher than the strike price that they were given for reasons that might have nothing whatsoever to do with their business decisions.

Another game that bosses play with options is called "rescission." When companies grant bosses rescission rights, bosses need not fret if share prices fall after they purchased stock through an exercise of their options. Rescission simply cancels the stock purchases. Bosses get their money back. Losses evaporate and so do the motivational benefits of pay for performance.[31]

One variant of these schemes that cannot even pretend to promote individual incentive occurs when bosses give one another option grants just before retirement. In 1999, for example, a bit before his April 30th retirement, Warner-Lambert gave its CEO a grant to purchase 392,000 shares of company stock, and Gillette's CEO retired a few months after receiving options for 800,000 shares.[32] As *Fortune* writer T. A. Stewart wrote, with privileges like these, options are "...charity, not capitalism.... Real capitalists put up real money...."[33]

Pensions themselves are often fashioned in a way that widens the gap between bosses and other employees. These plans commonly replace only 20 percent to 30 percent of pay that average workers received in their final year of employment, but between 50 percent and 100 percent of pay that senior executives received. They deny to most members of the workforce cost-of-living increases that are granted to their bosses. And, when years of service is part of the formula for calculating pensions, employees are generally bound by their actual work history, but bosses often get years, even decades, added to their count.

A twist on these schemes, used by FleetBoston Financial Corporation, occurred when its former CEO Terrence Murray retired. The company revised the retirement compensation formula so that it included stock option gains. This addition, regarded as unusual by compensation experts, enlarged his retirement income to $5.8 million from $2.7 million.[34]

At a time when companies are switching to plans that lower their liabilities, sometimes allowing them to reap many millions of dollars of over-funded benefits while lowering the average employee's pension income, they arrange for bosses' pensions to be calculated in the original, more lucrative ways. Ironically, even if bosses are propelled into excess prosperity by all these privileges, they needn't worry. Many have also given themselves a final special deal, available to no other employees: Their pension benefits can be swapped for life insurance trusts. The assets of these trusts can then be passed to a boss' heirs free of estate and income taxes. It's a sweet deal. As a Hershey Foods Corporation proxy statement says, "The purpose of the supplemental pension is to provide the executive and upper level management employees the means to continue their attained standard of living in retirement."[35]

The message is arrogant and one of exclusion. Restated it says, *The differences between us do not and need not conform to any rule of justice or fairness... We are a part of a class of people who have the power to give you rewards using rules from which we may choose to exempt ourselves. We will pay you what those rules require and pay ourselves according to the customs of compensation that are applicable to people like us.*

Privileges, Profits, and Shareholder Interest

Creating special financial preserves for privileged powerful bosses might have some justification if there were evidence that these perks boosted company performance. But evidence to the contrary comes from a Virginia Tech/Boston University study showing that companies using these tactics actually performed more poorly than competitors that did not.[36] And a study by William Gerard Sanders of Brigham Young University, investigating the activities of 250 large U.S. companies between 1991 and 1995, raises serious concern about how the award of options affects the business judgment of option holders.

Sanders' study showed that when top executives had large holdings in options, there was an increased occurrence of acquisitions, divestitures, and other activities that tend to produce short-term upswings in stock prices.[37] Bosses' self-interest has also been accused of being a contributing influence on bosses' support of questionable mergers and their dissemination of misleading information about business results.[38] Of course, these decisions are sometimes in a company's long-term interests—at other times, they are not. For example, under some circumstances, cutting costs for personnel, research and development, equipment, and plant, and reducing loyalty-enhancing customer discounts might improve both the current year's bottom line and stock prices at the cost of a toxic effect on a firm's longer term prospects.

After reviewing the use of the year's mega-grants of stock options, a 1999 *Fortune* magazine article concluded, "Companies like to argue that options tie the CEO's interests to those of stockholders and help push stocks up. Don't believe it.... Options are a free, no-lose proposition for CEOs." Citing a study by the *Analyst's Accounting Observer* newsletter, the article reports that 7 of the 10 companies granting the most options (measured in terms of options granted as a percentage of shares outstanding) over a three-year period *underperformed* the S&P 500.[39]

After investigating executive compensation in hundreds of companies, compensation expert Graef Crystal showed that there was little relationship between the compensation the executives received and organizational performance. Crystal began by grouping these companies into four categories: *Large*, with a market capitalization of between $1.6 and $87 billion and revenue between $201 million and $152 billion; *Midsize*, with capitalization between $434 million and $1.6 billion and revenue between $400,000 and $15.8 billion; *Small*, with capitalization between $133 million and $433 million and revenue between $70,000 and $7 billion; and *Ultra-small*, with capitalization between $1.4 million and $132 million and revenue between $10,000 and $1.1 billion.

Looking at executive compensation in each of these groups, he found that compensation is tied to neither company performance nor size. In *Large* companies, only 17.7 percent of executives' compensation was contingent on the firm's performance—almost 76 percent was discretionary. In the three other categories of companies, the story was even worse. The discretionary portion grew to approximately 82 percent in the *Midsize* companies, 89 percent in the *Small* companies, and 90 percent in the *Ultra-small* ones, while the portion tied to performance shrank to

15 percent, 10 percent, and 10 percent, respectively. Remarkably, a potentially fatal *we/they* boundary-creating event emerging from the smaller companies' data was that their CEOs' salaries often exceeded their organizations' after-tax earnings![40]

The devices misused by bosses to provide themselves with privileged means of compensation do more than make a mockery of the pay-for-performance rules that they so vigorously extol for others. These devices also threaten to harm shareholder interests. Consider the case of AT&T leader C. Michael Armstrong. According to reports, Mr. Armstrong received a risk-free deal with the company involving 224,561 shares of unrestricted stock. If, in October 2003, these shares are worth $10 million or more, they are his to dispose of as he sees fit. If they are worth less than $10 million—here you are probably expecting to read, "he makes less." Wrong!—*If they are worth less than $10 million*, the company will make up the difference.[41]

This deal unhinges pay from performance and diminishes AT&T stocks' shareholder value: If the 224,561 shares' worth falls below $10 million, then the company's reported obligation to pay the difference actually means that shareholder interests will be adversely affected by a decline in the company's assets equal to the amount that the company must pay to make up the difference between what the shares are worth and $10 million. Mention of this harmful effect is important because bosses often use protecting shareholder interests as a defense against accusations that their decisions are detrimental to employees' interests.

Shareholder interests are also adversely affected when companies issue excessively large option grants to their executives. A 1996 study by Investor Responsibility Research Center of more than 80 percent of the companies in the S&P 500 concluded that, because of options issued during that year, shareholders would lose an average of 9.2 percent of their ownership in companies where they were invested.[42] Options can also be used to distort a firm's earnings. During hearings that occurred in the U.S. Congress during February 2002, Jeffrey Skilling, Enron's former CEO, offered a one sentence explanation of how it's done: "Essentially what you do is issue stock options to reduce compensation expense, and therefore increase your profitability."[43]

These revelations might prompt you to learn about how executives are being compensated in companies in which you are a shareholder. Check the small print and read between the lines. By guaranteeing income no matter the performance, the measures being used by many of these bosses to reward themselves often raise costs to stockholders without providing any offsetting increase in their incentive to work well or wisely. Moreover, because the rules that employees' bosses force them to play by are different from the ones that the bosses apply to themselves, organization compensation schemes like the ones being discussed heighten employee alienation.

"Deferred compensation," as it is commonly practiced, is another good example of a scheme that has this bad effect. Deferred compensation, exclusively available to senior management, is not the same as the IRA, SRA, or 401K financial tools used by so many others in the workforce. For a start, the strict funding limits that government places on IRAs, SRAs, and 401Ks do not apply to deferred compensation schemes. Further, many companies help grow the assets that executives tuck away in deferred compensation plans by both guaranteeing a level of return and providing liberal matching funds.

For example, a *Wall Street Journal* article reported that in 2001, General Electric's plan permitted its former CEO, Jack Welch, to defer up to 90 percent of a $3.4 million salary, guaranteeing him a 12 percent return on the money that he deferred.[44] A similar arrangement in 1995 was augmented by a 3.5 percent matching contribution from General Electric and a promise to give 14 percent interest on the invested funds through 1999. Evidently, no similar deals were made to enhance most other employees' pension plans.[45]

Gross-ups are another nonsalary device exclusively available to senior-level bosses to protect their financial well-being when job loss occurs because control of a company changes. Essentially, gross-ups are a two- or three-year promise to pay an enhanced severance package (often three times annual salary plus bonus) and money to cover additional tax liabilities, if control of the bosses' employing company changes. Thus, this device creates two groups: One group, consisting of almost the entire workforce, possesses comparatively little job protection. It is completely at the mercy of the new organization. The second group is a small, elite force of executives who are crouching safely behind a financial bulwark that they built for themselves. This bulwark not only protects them from the ravages of job uncertainties in the newly controlled organization, it also might very well provide them with the financial incentive to shift control of the company, regardless of the shift's benefits for the firm, its employees, or the community.

Even when gross-ups are not proffered, some bosses receive acquisition/merger-related deals that are unavailable to other employees. When Deutsche Bank acquired Bankers Trust, Frank Newman, the Bankers

Trust CEO, purportedly got a deal that would have been hard for anyone to refuse: If he continued working, he was guaranteed $11 million a year for five years and, if he quit under the right conditions, he would also receive $11million a year for five years. He quit.

Richard Notebaert, former Ameritech CEO, got a similar deal when SBC acquired his company. He could have continued working. But if he quit, he was apparently entitled to receive a severance payment of approximately $15 million as well as a guaranteed $7 million a year for two years working as a consultant for the company. He quit, too.

BankAmerica's last CEO, David Coulter, also quit a month after NationsBank bought BankAmerica. He was reportedly guaranteed $5 million a year for life regardless of whether he stayed with the merged company. He chose to move on.[46]

Geoffrey Colvin, who wrote about these episodes in *Fortune* magazine, explained that all of these shenanigans are legal. What concerns this *Fortune* journalist is *how boards are spending shareholders' money*. That, and how it looks. *And*, concludes Mr. Colvin, *it looks rotten*. Deals like these make it easier for bosses to overlook future costs to their firm, its employees, and the surrounding community. The message that these deals send is an arrogant, alienating one saying, "I'm OK. You go look out for yourself."

Diligent stockholders searching company records should be able to easily discover other examples of perks for bosses that are not contingent on performance, detrimental to shareholders' financial interests, and alienating for employees. The *Wall Street Journal* reported that Robert Shaye, chairman and CEO of New Line Cinema, received a $750,000 unsecured, no-interest home loan from the company; Gerald Levin, CEO of Time Warner, had use of the company's three resort homes (two in Aspen and one in Acapulco) and six private planes; and SONY corporate executives enjoyed flights on one of its seven jets and dinners at the SONY club in New York, where meal charges were billed to work units.

In 1993, Baxter International Inc., a Chicago hospital supply company, cut 4,500 jobs and reported a net loss of $198 million. In that same year, Vernon Loucks, the company's CEO, was reported to have had $33,450 of club membership fees paid for him by the company, which also allegedly paid $79,600 for use of the company plane by Mr. Loucks and his family.[47]

Nor is economizing on health care plans a sacrifice that touches all organization members equally. Bosses are often exempt from health care plan limitations that their organizations impose on other employees.

For example, Charles Schwab Corporation's health care plan was reported to have elements that must surely communicate messages of exclusion. Employees are required to have an approved primary care physician authorize their referral to a specialist or hospital. Executives have unlimited choice. Employees pay for using doctors and hospitals outside the approved network. Executives have full coverage. Employees' maximum out-of-pocket expenses are as much as $2,500. For executives, it is zero. Atlantic Richfield, RJR Nabisco, SBC Communications (parent company of Southwestern Bell), and Gannett reportedly also have benefits in the health care plan provisions that are given to executives but denied to the rest of the workforce.

New York City's utility company, Con Edison, apparently has a plan that gives employees reimbursement for one pair of glasses each year and a shared hospital room. Company executives are reimbursed for two pairs of glasses and a private room.

When J. Peter Grace became ill, W.R. Grace (the company) provided $271,000 for "private nursing and related expense." Failure to report the benefit sparked an SEC investigation.[48]

Alltel, a telecommunications company based in Little Rock, Arkansas, continues to pay country club fees for its retired CEO, Joe Ford. For 10 years, IBM will do the same for its former CEO Louis Gerstner Jr., while it also covers his car and office expenses. And, FleetBoston Financial Corp. provides one-time CEO Terrence Murray with 150 hours per year of lifetime access to its company jet, funds for his home security system, a car and driver, and office with an assistant.[49]

Some, like Thomas Curley, publisher of *USA Today* (Gannett), justify these differences in health care protection saying, "It's deserved because we're responsible for bringing in the revenue and making the profits."[50] It is a flimsy justification. Lots of workers labor to bring in the profits, and there is considerable evidence that lots of bosses are paid for blunders and bungling, not for bringing in the profits.

Graef Crystal calculated the extent to which different factors accounted for the variation in the compensation that 279 executives received. Only 9 percent of their compensation was associated with shareholder return. About 16 percent of it was related to company size, and the low pay given to CEOs of utilities accounted for an additional 7 percent. This means that 68 percent of executive compensation was not tied to any factors whatsoever, much less to ones that reflected growth in profits. The simple truth is that executive compensation should not be interpreted as a carefully crafted reflection of performance.

Bonuses for Bungling

The consequences for employees' *we/they* boundaries are particularly grim when bosses appear to be compensating themselves for failures. According to reports, in July 1997, AT&T nudged President John R. Walters out of the company after he was on the job for only nine months. His severance package was estimated to be to $26 million. Its size is surprising in light of AT&T Director Walter Elisha's comment that Mr. Walters "lacked the intellectual leadership to lead AT&T."[51]

In July 1997, after approximately 18 months on the job, Chairman and CEO of Apple Computer Gilbert F. Amelio was ushered out of his position when "he failed to turn around the troubled company."[52] During his tenure, the company's losses were estimated to be $2 billion. Accounts about his exact severance differ, placing it at either $6.7 million or $9.2 million. In either case, it seems like a lot for someone who apparently accomplished so little.

Between 1993 and 1996, the price of Time Warner's stock declined 15.3 percent, although the S&P 500 rose 58.8 percent. Reports make it evident that the company's anomalous negative performance did not hurt CEO Gerald Levin's compensation, which benefited from a $4 million bonus in each of those years and a $6.7 million bonus in 1998, when Time Warner's stock price finally rose.[53]

For about a decade, until 1998, Dr. William J. Catacosinos was CEO of Long Island Lighting Company, known as LILCO. When he took over the company, it was saddled with debt that was incurred when the utility built the Shoreham nuclear power plant. Dr. Catacosinos disposed of both the Shoreham facility and the debt in a deal with New York State that transferred the costs to customers, causing them to pay the nation's second-highest utility rates. (At the time, Hawaii's customers topped the list.)[54]

Most troubling are assertions that while he was juggling LILCO's problems, Dr. Catacosinos was also " laying the foundation for a lucrative departure from the utility...."[55] If that was his strategy, then it worked. Dr. Catacosinos left LILCO with a package said to be worth $42 million. It is especially troubling that both his departure package and the pay he received prior to his leaving seem inconsistent with other indices of the utility's performance. During his watch, in addition to ratepayers' paying very large bills, LILCO's shareholders received substandard returns. Including stock price appreciation and reinvested dividends, their total return was 451 percent, whereas the average return to stockholders who had invested in comparable utilities was 613 percent.

Despite this performance, Dr. Catacosinos' salary and bonus in 1997, the year before he left LILCO, was $1.9 million, reportedly twice as much as the median amount paid to eight CEOs of comparable utilities. Strangely, before his departure, and despite LILCO's comparatively poor performance, Dr. Catacosinos received two performance awards: one, in stock, for $742,500, and the other in cash amounting to $743,750.

These antics caught Graef Crystal's attention. We can imagine Mr. Crystal sighing audibly when he said, "It's hard for me to recall ever seeing a set of contracted pay arrangements that were so stacked in favor of the executive and against shareholders."

Of course, it is always possible to claim that without Dr. Catacosinos' work, LILCO's financial condition would have been even worse. But, without evidence of a statistically significant reversal of a downward trend, this is a claim that should be unequivocally rejected as the basis for reward. If it were to be used as a valid justification for compensation, then using that same reasoning should also permit organizations to *reduce* executive compensation, despite an upward turn in the indices, claiming that if someone other than the executive (say Dr. Catacosinos) had been at the helm, the company's financial position would have been still better. Since that does not seem like a rationale that most senior managers would accept, they should not be given license to use the equally flimsy *it could have been worse* justification to defend their pay for nonperformance.

CEO Robert Allen's pay and performance at AT&T have also caused some to ask how a "...Chief Executive could earn a fortune while delivering only mediocre returns to the owners."[56] In 1995, AT&T just about broke even. Subsequently, the company threatened dismissal of 40,000 employees and gave CEO Robert Allen $5.2 million in options. Two years later, in 1997, AT&T's apparent pay-for-nonperformance was again the subject of criticism. Despite questionable individual performance, dismal profits, and continued downsizing, AT&T's senior team members received substantial raises. One commentator pointed out that "AT&T has been criticized for several strategic moves in the last couple of years, including its entry into local phone services, Internet, and international alliances. Yet the company paid its strategy chief, Executive Vice President John C. Petrullo, $908,133, a 21 percent raise in salary and bonus over 1996."[57]

The story did not end with Mr. Petrullo. AT&T's consumer services' revenue declined, losing 7 percent in fourth quarter 1996, yet the consumer chief earned $896,367, which translates into a 37 percent raise. And other companies reportedly outstripped AT&T in installing advanced optic lines and other technology, but the computer operations chief received $883,667, equivalent to a 62 percent raise.

"The Michaels' Tale," with its special twist, raises unique questions about the pay-for-nonperformance dilemma. Michael Ovitz was hired as head of the Disney Company, joining an old friend, Disney chairman Michael Eisner. Evidently, the Michaels were better as acquaintances than as coworkers.[58] Unable to either resolve differences or live with them, Ovitz soon parted company with Eisner. Easing his leaving was a reputed cash settlement of $50 million and stock options worth $40 million. Wondering why he received such a large parting package leads to some bewildering possibilities: If Ovitz was competent, why did the board permit Chairman Eisner to pay so much to get rid of him? And, if he was *not* competent, then should he have received a $90 million settlement?

Events like the ones that involved the Michaels, Robert Allen, Dr. William Catacosinos, John Walters, and Gilbert Amelio leave the workforce and other observers with a distinct impression that bosses are being richly rewarded for their blundering. When other employees believe that their own blundering is more likely to cause them grief, rather than the benefits that these bosses enjoy, the effect on them is heightened alienation and diminished organizational identity.

Therefore, let us applaud Dr. William H. Joyce, CEO of Union Carbide, whose compensation package is very different from those of the Michaels, Robert Allen, Dr. Catacosinos, John Walters, Gilbert Amelio, and many other members of the management elite. A 1998 report explained that Dr. Joyce's salary of $800,000 depended on Union Carbide earning $4 a share in the year 2000. Sixteen members of Dr. Joyce's senior team joined him by accepting compensation packages that made 65 percent of their salaries contingent on the firm's performance. If, in the interim, their leadership really excelled, causing Union Carbide's earnings to reach $4.75 per share in 1999 and 2000, then members of this senior team could earn as much as eight times the portion of salary that they put at risk.[59]

As an incentive scheme, Union Carbide's plan has merit for two reasons. First, it ties portions of this executive team's compensation to *measurable performance targets* that bear a more obvious connection to work effort than overall share price. (In this case earnings, but in other circumstances the contingent standard used could be technological progress, workforce development, or productivity.) Second, the plan has merit because of the potential size of the rewards that can be earned. Incentive portions of compensation that are small increments to large bases are public relations gimmicks with little influence on work behavior. In order to become a meaningful incentive, the portion must be large and clearly linked to work effort.[60]

In addition to its incentive value for members of Mr. Joyce's senior management team, Union Carbide's plan sends the firm's employees an important inclusion-inducing message. Assuming that the performance goals are a stretch, by foregoing guarantees of payment, this executive team sends a message to the workforce that says *we're in this with you*, rather than, *we'll bet* your *career on our business decisions, but not our own.*

Recruitment and Retention

In addition to the *we make the profits* defense, *executive recruitment* and *retention* are commonly offered as excuses for using one set of compensation rules for bosses and an entirely different set for everyone else. The claim is that if these special, exclusive inducements were not offered, firms would watch helplessly as their competitors hired the most talented individuals. Evidence proves that this claim is false.

A two-year comparison of more than 100 companies that repriced options with others that did not actually showed that turnover for option recipients not only didn't improve, it worsened! Bosses' defections were two to four times greater in companies that repriced than in those with no repricing policy.[61]

Of course, like so many self-fulfilling prophecies, the fear of losing talent to competitors has become self-reinforcing, because one byproduct of the *we-must-give-special-inducements* solution to recruitment and retention is a constantly escalating, ever more tempting package of compensation for senior management.

Now that the cycle of escalation is underway, breaking its momentum is difficult. Talent might actually go elsewhere (unless other organizations also decide to get off the bandwagon), peers are likely to be angry with anyone who attempts to break the cycle, threatening the growth of their future incomes, and ending the cycle will diminish the size of future raises. In sum, organization bosses' self-interest now works against whatever motives they once might have had for de-escalating this self-fulfilling prophecy: *Everyone is doing it; therefore, we must also.*

The problem is that the people influencing compensation decisions are frequently part of a group that benefits from the rising tide of compensation. For example, senior executives often either directly select their companies' outside compensation consultants or provide influential advice to Boards of Directors' compensation committees about which consultants should be used.[62] Given this level of involvement by potential beneficiaries of the consultants' inputs, no one should be surprised to learn that companies shop around for accommodating consultants. In fact, evidence from a study of 1,197 companies conducted by the Investor Responsibility Research Center shows that 43 percent of their Boards of Directors' compensation committees include members with existing or prior *business* affiliations with the company.[63] Add to that percentage an unspecified number of other directors who secretly desire *future* business affiliations with the company. What emerges is a volume of circumstantial evidence that accuses senior managers of using their positions of influence to bestow on themselves privileges that are completely unavailable to other members of the workforce. And so the gap grows.

Ironically, evidence about the effects of large recruitment inducements on executive retention shows that this *"we'll-buy-their-loyalty"* strategy sows the seeds of its failure. A 1996 *Executive Compensation Reports* study reveals that, despite large recruitment bonuses, within two years after they were hired, fewer than half the recruited executives remained with the company that had hired them.[64] And, in Silicon Valley, a 1999 report showed that each year, companies lose about one-fifth of their workforce to rivals who have simply upped the financial allure of their recruitment packages.[65] Perhaps, when companies tout self-interest as the dominant reason for joining them, they are creating a motivational climate that inclines those whom they have hired to quickly migrate toward the next highest bidder.

What's Fair?

It would be a pleasure if, at this point, it were possible to present a formula defining how the ratio of executive compensation to average workforce compensation affects messages of inclusion and exclusion. But, alas, that is not possible. The best that is available is a crude general principle: If they are to be messages of inclusion, causing employees to see the organization as *we* rather than *they*, then the rules governing the distribution of compensation in organizations must be judged by employees as fair.

When most of a company's bosses seem to be greedily feathering their nests at employee and shareholder expense, enforcing rules that protect them while leaving others in jeopardy, or making midstream, self-serving changes in the rules by which rewards are distributed, their actions will be judged as unfair. In short, compensation practices tend to be judged as "fair" when they have the following qualities: They are *consistent* (applied in the same way over time and across groups); *bias free* (without privileges or disadvantages to some that are not rationally work related); *accurate* (based on credible data); *correctable* (possessing an accessible and trusted means for exercising influence when disputes arise); *representative of varied interests* (structured in a way that clearly reflects the varying wishes of organization members); and *ethical* (in accord with accepted codes of conduct for managing social transactions).[66]

Unfair compensation systems, lacking these qualities, become messages of exclusion that contribute to employee alienation because bosses are saying, "*we* are treated fairly, but *they* need not be." Research has repeatedly documented that unfair systems are a cause of poor work performance, lack of cooperation, higher rates of theft, and both physical and psychological withdrawal.[67]

Although the six identified attributes of fair systems can serve as useful guidelines for examining any organization's compensation practices, because they lack objective specifications, they are vulnerable to self-serving errors of subjective judgment. More likely than not, bosses who have invented, endorsed, implemented, and profited from the practices will judge them more favorably than will employees who are merely the practices' passive recipients.[68]

Ire, rather than identification with the organization, is likely to be the workforce's response to violations of the six attributes of fairness. This might very well be what happened at the Columbia Falls Aluminum Company some years ago. According to reports, in 1985, the company struck a deal with employees wherein a promise to share company profits was exchanged for employees' acceptance of a 15 percent pay cut. Although Columbia Falls was making no profit at the time, the looming threat of a shutdown made this deal an acceptable option.

Perhaps the promised sharing of profits succeeded as an incentive to improved work behavior because, one year later, the company recorded a profit. Subsequently, B.W. Duker, Columbia Falls Aluminum's principle owner, shared the earnings with employees, living up to his promise to them that "a dollar in your pocket is a dollar in mine."[69] After that auspicious beginning, however, Mr. Duker and his minority partner, Mr. Jerome Broussard, apparently introduced a unilateral change in the rules for compensation by giving themselves approximately $3 for every $1 they gave to employees.

Mr. Duker and Mr. Broussard managed this distribution by channeling the Columbia Falls' profits to Eural, a shell company in the Cayman Islands. Their claim was that nothing wrong had occurred. They were using this offshore company merely because it was a lure for customers who were not favorably disposed toward doing business with Columbia Falls Aluminum.

Employees eventually demanded what they believed was fairly theirs. During the protracted court battle that followed, Mr. Duker and Mr. Broussard offered to settle employee claims for $12 million (it was rejected), $50 million (also rejected), and $97 million (which was accepted).

There is a small epitaph to this exhibition of apparent managerial avarice. According to one report, in 1998, Mr. Duker was being sued by one of his former lawyers who claimed that he had not been paid a $3 million bonus that was fairly his because he held the final settlement with employees to under $100 million.[70]

Greed is an enemy of fairness. It encourages inconsistency and bias and motivates selective use of data, defensiveness, dogmatism, neglect of others' views, and even unethical behavior. A major, frequently unrecognized problem with bosses' greed is what the act says about their regard for other employees. Bosses' acts of greed not only adversely affect reward distribution, they also communicate to employees/victims that the greedy bosses do not regard their well being as a matter of concern. Greedy behavior is inconsistent with emotional attachment. *We* do not selfishly harm one of *us*. Employees who are targets of bosses' greed reasonably infer that their greedy bosses view them as *they,* not *we.* Recognizing that their bosses have excluded them, employees respond by excluding. In their mind's eye, the organization icon is moved away from the *we* side of the boundary, further into *they* territory. Once employing organizations are categorized as *they,* the organization golden rule is inapplicable, there is diminished concern with organization outcomes, and employees are psychologically free to pursue selfish, self-interested motives.

Rewarding *We*

Compensation schemes can be a structural means for remedying selfish self-interest at every level of organization. Once, when asked whether he was motivated by stock options, General Electric's now retired CEO, Jack Welch, replied "Absolutely."[71] According to reports, Mr. Welch practices what he preaches. He set and monitored clear performance goals for his direct reports, expecting them to do the same with their own direct reports. Salary increase, bonuses, and stock option grants were subsequently linked to attainment of these goals. "The result," according to one observer, "is a cascading down of the objective performance measures and performance-appraisal-based rewards for performance."[72]

The motivational effects of properly implemented financial schemes are not idiosyncratic to GE and Jack Welch. A study conducted by the United States General Accounting Office shows that, in comparison to their corporate counterparts, companies with compensation programs that give employees a personal investment in organization outcomes experience higher profits, more income, and greater commitment from employees. These companies also experience less in the way of grievances, absenteeism, and turnover.[73]

Confirmation of the General Accounting Office's findings was obtained from at least two other, more recent, studies. One, a 1997 Wyatt study, reported that shareholder returns were greater for companies with incentive plans linking performance to compensation.[74] And a 1993 U.S. Department of Labor study reviewing 27 econometric investigations reported that productivity was between 3 percent and 5 percent higher in companies with profit-sharing plans than in comparable firms lacking them. When one firm, United Technologies, extended profit sharing to over 1,500 nonunion employees working in a manufacturing plant in North Berwick, Maine, there was "breathtaking improvement" amounting to a payout of $1,500 per employee.[75]

Firms with *profit sharing* plans, as the term implies, use profitability indices to determine reward distributions. In contrast, those with *gain sharing* plans use increases in productivity, rather than profit, as the metric for determining distributions. The evidence for the benefits of gain sharing, however, is equally positive. In one study of 38 companies using gain sharing, the average gain in productivity was better than 22 percent.[76]

McKay Nursery, an agricultural company based in Waterloo, Wisconsin, recognizes the value of a properly sculpted employee compensation plan. The company employs 60 full-time workers and up to 100 part-timers. In 1984, it converted to an ESOP (Employee Stock Option Plan), allowing *all* workers to participate in the company's profit sharing plan. That even migrant part-timers could become eligible for participation is not surprising in light of McKay's history. Long before similar firms did so, McKay offered overtime pay to migrant workers and, seven years before it adopted an ESOP, McKay permitted migrant workers to join the profit sharing plan that existed at that time.[77]

McKay's president, Griff Mason, said, "At first, the primary motivation was idealistic. But it's also pragmatic. These migrants are critical to making the place work. Agricultural work is not glamorous, and it helps to attract people." To which Corey Rosen, Director of the National Conference for Employee Ownership, added, "McKay's idea is that if you treat these people like human beings and they come back every year, you cut training costs, you get loyal employees, and you get your pick of workers."

President Mason's and Director Rosen's observations receive support from Gilberto Heredia, a migrant who worked his way into a full-time job, as did his wife, Eva Heredia. Mr. Heredia said that McKay's benefits "make you want to get involved with the company and do the best you can."[78] These words reveal how compensation schemes affect employees' emotional attachment to employers and their pro-organization work behavior. I bet Mr. Heredia would turn out organization lights that were burning wastefully.

Sadly, despite all this affirming empirical and anecdotal evidence, in 1998 only 5 million employees in the United States were receiving stock options (about 4 percent of the workforce), and perhaps as few as 10 million others (about 7 percent of the work force) worked in ESOPs, sharing corporate profits.[79] After surveying 1,800 companies, William H. Mercer, Inc. reported in 1999 that, at best, about one-half provided non-management and nonsales personnel with compensation contingent on performance.[80]

Some bosses read these results, get excited, but miss the point entirely. They seem to believe that if they merely introduce a compensation plan linking employee outcome to performance, all will be well, regardless of how the plan is introduced or the characteristics of the organization setting into which the plan is imbedded. Existing evidence says that they are wrong. The beneficial emotional attachment that can be stimulated by cooperatively structured compensation plans happens in firms that introduce these financial schemes along with other inclusion-inducing organization supports. Injecting these schemes amid an army of exclusion-inducing personnel practices does not have the same positive consequence.

A 1988 study published by the United States General Accounting Office proves the point. It reports that productivity was 52 percent higher in companies that combined employee ownership through 401Ks and ESOPs with some form of participation in management, than it was in companies lacking this combination.[81] Employees might be happy for the chance to receive more compensation when these schemes are installed into otherwise inhospitable organization surroundings, but years of research evidence declares that their pleasure is not going to dull their response to bosses' underlying intent. If surrounding circumstances cause the plan to be perceived as an effort to manipulate, coerce, or ingratiate, rather than as part of a genuine effort to involve, employees' responses to the pay system are going to be adverse. Performance might improve until workers' antagonism spurs them to find a way to beat the system, but the compensation plan's perceived ulterior motives will ultimately undermine employees' initiative, commitment, loyalty, and any of the other benefits of employees' organizational identity.

If evidence about the benefits of inclusion-inducing compensation plans is so consistent and clear, then why is their use so meager? Why are these plans available to such a small portion of the workforce? Why does an estimated 90 percent of the workforce report having had an experience with an abusive boss?[82] Why do so many bosses proclaim the benefits of participation, while simultaneously sending messages communicating that *their* subordinates lack the competence necessary to participate in problem solving?

Profit and *power* are two easy, obvious, and correct answers. Accumulating profit and power gives bosses tangible benefits as well as the freedom to act as they wish, unconstrained by the needs or concerns of subordinates. But there is a third "P" in this trilogy of perverse motives: *Prestige*.

Human tendencies to make social comparisons encourage bosses to further boost their status. As the *haves'* riches and power grow, it inflates their self-esteem and deflates their esteem for others in the workforce, who the *haves* view as lacking the stuff it takes to reach such exalted heights. In short, besides the concrete quality of life's benefits that profit and power provide, bosses accumulate these two *P*s as a means of enhancing their prestige and sense of personal worth. Thus, bosses' misbehavior is caused by social greed as well as financial greed.

It is tempting to claim that this explanation is too psychological. Why not simply believe that bosses' greedy financial self-interest is what deters them from making more widespread use of inclusion-inducing compensation plans? After all, both tangible rewards and power ease some of life's hardships. To the bosses involved, it might reasonably appear that the more of each they give away to other employees, the less they will have left for themselves. Perhaps it is no more than an uncomplicated case of *more is better*.

This alternative explanation might be convincing if bosses did not behave with similar arrogance when it comes to showing other members of the workforce respect and recognition. As the next two chapters demonstrate, those are occasions during which financial gain is out of the picture, and both data and common sense shout to us all that bosses' messages of inclusion would yield more organizational benefit than their messages of exclusion.

[1] Fisher, A. B. "Readers on pay: Many are angry, a few think the big guy is worth it." *Fortune* (June 8, 1998): 276.

[2] Ibid.

[3] In fairness, it is important to add that in comparison to CEOs of similar size companies with equivalent shareholder performance for 1996–1998, Mr. Gerstner's pay was among the lowest according to R. Abelson "Silicon valley aftershocks." *New York Times* (April 4, 1999): Bu1, Bu9.

[4] Johnston, D. C. "Bountiful harvest seen in managerial suites." *New York Times* (January 9, 2000): 6.

[5] Lublin, J. S. "Net envy." *Wall Street Journal*, (April 6, 2000): R1 and R3.

[6] Leonhardt, D. "For the boss, happy days are still here." *New York Times* (April 1, 2001): Bu1, Bu8.

[7] Leonhardt, D. "Did pay incentives cut both ways?" *New York Times* (April 7, 2002): Bu3, Bu6–Bu7.

[8] Belson, K. "Learning how to talk about salary in Japan." *New York Times* (April 7, 2002): Bu1, Bu12.; Cassidy, J. "Who killed the middle class?" *The New Yorker* (October 16, 1995): 113–124; Colvin, G. "The great CEO pay heist." *Fortune* (June 25, 2001): 64–92.

[9] Egan, T. "Strikers at Boeing point to top management's stock options." *New York Times* (November 25, 1995): 6.

[10] Greenhouse, S. "Deeper shade of blue collar." *New York Times* (August 8, 1997): L26.

[11] Champy, J. A. "Business 101, the hard way." *New York Times* (August 16, 1997): A21. Italics added.

[12] Herbert, B. "A workers' rebellion." *New York Times* (August 7, 1997): A31.

[13] Charlotte, North Carolina's steel maker, Nucor Corporation, has a similar pattern. Typically, 40 percent of production workers' income is base pay, and 60 percent is from bonuses contingent on performance.

[14] Jacobs, K. "The real thing." *Wall Street Journal* (April 9, 1998): R11.

[15] Dumaine, B. "A knockout year." *Fortune* (July 25, 1994): 94–102.

[16] Lublin, J. S. "Pay for no performance." *Wall Street Journal* (April 9, 1998): R1, R4.

[17] Ibid.

[18] Leonhardt, "For the boss, happy days are still here."

[19] Oppel, R. A. Jr. "Option foe is not so lonely now." *New York Times* (April 7, 2002): Bu2.

[20] "Work Week." *Wall Street Journal* (January 18, 2000): A1.

[21] Dobrzynski, J. H. "New road to riches is paved with options." *New York Times* (March 30, 1997): F1, F10–F11.

[22] Tully, S. "Raising the bar." *Fortune* (June 8, 1998): 272–278.

[23] "Work Week." *Wall Street Journal* (January 18, 2000): A1.

[24] Morgenson, G. "It's time for investors to start acting like owners." *New York Times* (March 24, 2002): Bu1.

[25] Strom, S. "Even last year, the option spigot was wide open." *New York Times* (February 3, 2002): B1.

[26] Tully, S. "Raising the bar." *Fortune* (June 8, 1998): 272.

[27] Leonhardt, D. "The letter, if not the spirit on options pricing." *New York Times* (April 1, 2000): Bu8.

[28] Lublin, J. S. "A better way?" *Wall Street Journal* (April 9, 1998): R12.

[29] Norris, F. "Stock options are faulted by Buffet." *New York Times* (March 11, 2002): C1, C7.

[30] Colvin, G. "A CEO's pay goes negative." *Fortune* (March 15, 1999): 35.

[31] Norris, F. "New corporate perk. If the stock falls, cancel purchases." *New York Times* (January 26, 2001): C1.

[32] Colter, G. "It's a banner year for CEO pay." *Fortune* (April 26, 1999): 422–424.

[33] Stewart, T. A. "Will the real capitalist please stand up?" *Fortune* (May 11, 1998): 189–190.

[34] Lublin, J. S. "Under the radar." *Wall Street Journal* (April 11, 2002): B7, B10.

[35] Schultz, E. E. "As firms pare pensions for most, they boost those for executives." *Wall Street Journal* (May 20, 2001): A1, A8.

[36] "As some stock prices sag, CEOs win, public loses." *USA Today* (April 29, 1997): 12.

[37] Bryant, A. "Feeding the new work ethic." *New York Times* (April 19, 1998): WK1, WK4.

[38] Leonhardt, D. "Tell the good news, then cash in." *New York Times* (April 7, 2002): Bu1, Bu12; Sorkin, A. R. "Those sweet trips to the merger mall." *New York Times* (April 7, 2002): Bu1, Bu12.

[39] Colter, "It's a banner year for CEO pay."

[40] Dobrzynski, J. H. "Getting what they deserve?" *New York Times* (February 22, 1996): D1, D9.

[41] Lublin, J. S. "Pay for no performance." *Wall Street Journal* (April 9, 1998): R1, R4; Silverman, R. E. "Heads I win, tails I win." *Wall Street Journal* (April 6, 2000): R4.

[42] Dobrzynski, "New road to riches is paved with options."

[43] Hitt, G. and J. M. Schlesinger. "Stock options come under fire in wake of Enron's collapse." *Wall Street Journal* (March 26, 2002): A1, A8.

[44] Lublin, J. S. "Under the radar."

[45] Drew, C. and Johnston, D. C. "Special tax breaks enrich savings of many in ranks of management." *New York Times* (October 13, 1996): 1, 36–37.

[46] Colvin, G. "Value driven." *Fortune* (February 21, 2000): 78.

[47] "In a cost-cutting era, many CEOs enjoy imperial perks." *Wall Street Journal* (March 7, 1995): B1, B6.

[48] All the preceding material about health care plans is from Myerson, A. R. "Executives cradled while medical benefits are cut for rank and file." *New York Times* (March 17, 1996): F1, F13.

[49] Leonhardt, D. "Perks make life comfortable, even in retirement." *New York Times* (April 7, 2002): Bu5; Lublin, J. S. "Under the radar." *Wall Street Journal* (April 11, 2002): B7, B10.

[50] Myerson, "Executives cradled while medical benefits are cut for rank and file." F13.

[51] Bryant, A. "How the mighty have fallen, and sometimes profited anyway." *New York Times* (January 5, 1998): D4.

[52] Bryant, "How the mighty have fallen, and sometimes profited anyway."; Lublin, J. S. "Pay for non performance." *Wall Street Journal* (April 9, 1998): R1, R4.

[53] Bryant, A. "Executive cash machine." *New York Times* (November 8, 1998): Bu1, Bu12.

[54] Sachs, S. "Joined in a corporate marriage, but divided by style and vision." *New York Times* (August 1, 1998): B2.

[55] Bryant, A. "LILCO 'golden parachute' woven in advance." *New York Times* (June 11, 1998): B1, B4.

[56] Lowenstein, R. "Is Chairman Allen of AT&T overpaid?" *Wall Street Journal* (February 29, 1996): C1.

[57] Keller, J. J. "AT&T handsomely rewarded top brass." *Wall Street Journal* (March 27, 1998): A3, A6.

[58] Rosenthal, A. M. "Hardtack for the journey." *New York Times* (December 17, 1996): A25.

[59] Lublin, J. S. "Pay for no performance."

[60] Lawler, E. E. III. *Strategic Pay*. San Francisco: Jossey-Bass Publishers, 1990.

[61] Morgenson, C. "Dispelling the myth that options help shareholders." *New York Times* (July 29, 2001): Bu1.

[62] Lawler, E. A. *Rewarding Excellence*. San Francisco: Jossey-Bass Publishers, 2000.

[63] Bryant, A. "Executive cash machine." *New York Times* (November 8, 1998): Bu1, Bu12; Strauss, G. "Do conflicts cloud the objectivity of corporation boards?" *USA Today* (March 5, 2002): 1–2.

[64] Thomas, P. "Business Bulletin." *Wall Street Journal* (October 29, 1996): A1.

[65] Abelson, R. "Silicon Valley aftershocks." *New York Times* (April 4, 1999): Bu1, Bu9.

[66] Folger, R. and R. Cropanzo. *Organizational Justice and Human Resource Management*. California: Sage, 1998.

[67] Ibid.

[68] Greenberg, J. *The Quest for Justice on the Job.* Thousand Oaks, CA: Sage, 1996.

[69] Robbins, J. "A broken pact and a $97 million payday." *New York Times* (April 19, 1998): Bu1, Bu11.

[70] Ibid.

[71] Carley, W. M. "GE Chairman defends pay, stresses quality." *Wall Street Journal* (April 24, 1997): A4.

[72] Lawler, E. E. III. *Strategic Pay.* San Francisco: Jossey-Bass Publishers, 1990.

[73] Preiwisch, C. F. "GAO study on productivity sharing programs." In V. M. Buckler and Y. K. Shetty (Eds.) *Productivity Improvement.* New York: AMACOM, 1981.

[74] Kay, I. T. "High CEO pay helps US economy thrive." *Wall Street Journal* (February 23, 1998): A22.

[75] White, J. B. and J. S. Lublin. "Some companies try to rebuild loyalty." *Wall Street Journal* (September 27, 1996): B1, B6.

[76] Casio, W. F. "Guide to responsible restructuring." US Department of Labor. Office of the American Workplace, 1995.

[77] Kaufman, J. "Sharing the wealth." *Wall Street Journal* (April 9, 1998): R10.

[78] Ibid.

[79] Ibid.

[80] Karr, A. R. "Work Week." *Wall Street Journal* (April 6, 1999): A1.

[81] Richardson, P. "Making workers act like owners." *Institutional Investor* 29 (November, 1995): 31.

[82] Hornstein, H. A. *Brutal Bosses and Their Prey.* New York: Riverhead Books, 1996.

3

THE SECOND R—
RESPECT:
WORKING WITH
AUTHORITY

Jack Hartnett is a demanding boss. He has high standards and expects
them to be met. He is also a boss whose management style reveals that
when it comes to employee inclusion, identity, and *we/they* boundaries, he
understands that what you give is what you get: *We* begets *we* and *they*
begets *they*. This understanding gives Mr. Hartnett an advantage over a
surprisingly large number of other bosses. In his hands, respect for
employees becomes a competitive advantage. The proof is in the profits.[1]

Mr. Hartnett, age 40-something, is president of D.L. Rogers
Corporation. The company operates 54 drive-in restaurants franchised
from Sonia Corporation. In 1997, these restaurants produced $44 million
in revenues for Mr. Hartnett's company. That dollar volume put Mr.
Hartnett's restaurants about 18 percent above Sonia Corporation's average
per-store revenues, which were themselves above the industry's average.

The boss behind this performance hardly comes across as a warm,
cuddly pushover. One of his personal guidelines proclaims *I want people*

to do what I want them to do. Backing that demand is his list of commandments, including the infamous eighth, which is "I will tell you one time." Of course, this is not all there is to Mr. Hartnett's management style. If it were, then his company's managers probably would *not* remain in his employ for approximately 9 years and his supervisors for over 12 years, when job tenure in the rest of the industry averages in the neighborhood of only 2 and 3.5 years, respectively.

The plus that transforms Jack Hartnett from an *excludoboss* to an *includoboss* was captured by a faculty member at the University of Southern California's Marshall School of Business, Professor Jay Conger. He said, "The better business leaders understand that employees are coming to their jobs looking for a sense of community, family, spiritual fulfillment, and a place to develop themselves."[2] Mr. Hartnett builds this sense of community within D.L. Rogers Corporation by the way in which he dispenses compensation (**R**ewards), organizes work (**R**ecognition), and exercises his authority (**R**espect), the three **R**s of organizational life.

Key employees at D.L. Rogers Corporation have a financial stake in the business. After 18 months, managers' bonuses are based on a share of the business' net profits, and after three years, managers are permitted to purchase a 1 percent share in a new store. Similarly, after some time on the job, supervisors can become eligible for bonuses that are pegged to their store's net profits.

Mr. Hartnett organizes work in ways that facilitate team development. Among his many efforts in this regard are quarterly gatherings of supervisors. These commonly begin with a Hartnett-style outward-bound experience in which success depends on team members' coordinated efforts. One supervisor pointed directly to their positive effects on employee inclusion by saying, "These things bring all of us together and build camaraderie and teamwork."[3]

Most importantly, Mr. Hartnett is a boss who shows his respect for employees by standing with, not above, the workforce. One observer pointed out that "… he's not above choosing the grimiest of jobs out of a distinctly unglamorous lot." At one store opening, for example, after a 15-hour day, Jack Hartnett prepared a taco salad for 20 workers. An unusual illustration of just how well he has done in building community occurred one night, at 3:30 A.M. to be exact, when a group of supervisors awakened him for a poker game, causing one commentator to observe "their behavior showed just how much they consider him … one of them."

Taco salads and poker games are merely one boss's way of sending messages of inclusion; imitation of that way is not necessarily the answer.

Instead, bosses everywhere would be better advised to think of Jack Hartnett's efforts and then ask themselves, *What symbolic equivalents should become part of our organization, and what symbolic opposites exist within our organization that require removal?*

Craig Weatherup, once Pepsi's chief of global beverage operations, is like Mr. Hartnett in that he is also known as both a tough, successful executive *and* a nice guy. During his watch, Pepsi's domestic sales doubled, operating profits tripled, the bottling operation was restructured, radically new products were successfully brought to market, operations were closed, and employees were dismissed. Through it all, what Mr. Weatherup said showed that he understood why organizations must send messages that build rather than sever employees' emotional attachment to their employers. "We have 60,000 employees" he said, "I meet very few of them, but I need that entire group to believe in me...." Mr. Weatherup confessed that he would like to see Pepsi's stock price higher, but "if we get to $55, and the difference between getting from $55 to $60 is to lose our humanity, I wouldn't want to do it."[4]

We Rules

Clearly, exercising authority is not the cause of employee alienation. And workforce affiliation does not occur simply because bosses observe social etiquette, use warm, friendly tones, or maintain a pleasant countenance. Hierarchies can be steep, gently sloping, or flat. Employees can be located nearer a hierarchy's top or bottom. None of those matters as much as bosses' messages defining who is inside the organization's circle of *we* and who is an outside member of *they*.

Regardless of the intention behind them, boss behaviors always contain messages of inclusion or exclusion. Behaviors that conform to expectations created by the psychological golden rule of organizations (*Harming you becomes difficult for me because the two of us are part of we*) carry messages of inclusion, and they build employees' organizational identification. Those that violate rule-generated expectations bear messages of exclusion that sever employees' identification.

According to the rule, *we* group members should *trust* other *we* group members. As members of the same community *we* should be disinclined to harm one another. Delegation and other managerial means of granting employees' autonomy are ways of saying, "I trust that you will do the right thing even in the absence of surveillance." It is a message of inclusion.

Micromanagement signals mistrust, sending a message of exclusion to employees. It says, *Close control is needed precisely because employees are not part of* our *community of* we. *Increased freedom for* them *will not release well-intended work behavior. Because* they *cannot be relied upon to do the right thing, achieving organization goals requires that* we *maintain tight surveillance and close control over* them.

We group members are also empathetically aware of other members' pleasure and pain. We *care about* us. When there are bonds of *we,* one member's plight or pleasure is capable of stimulating another's passions. We see it happen when moviegoers weep, fear, or feel relief for characters on the screen. And we see it when family members experience one another's struggles or successes as if they were their own. That is what identification is all about. It is at the heart of the psychological golden rule of organizations. Bosses who exhibit callused indifference to workers' tragedies and successes are sending rule-contrary messages of exclusion. They don't appear to care about a family member's death or a child's graduation. Employees' long-term illnesses or their struggles with that morning's traffic problems seem to be of no concern to these bosses. Perfunctory, schooled social charm might produce a stereotypic "tsk-tsk" or "atta-boy," but their eyes and the aftermath of their behavior reveal a truth: They don't really care. They are unconnected. Employees are outside their circle, one of *them*, not one of *us*.

We say of such bosses, *they lack a sense of humanity—they're without feelings, caring, or understanding—they're above it all.* These bosses treat their employees instrumentally. To them, subordinates are no more than expendable tools whose worth is largely determined by their usefulness for the task at hand. "It is all business," say these bosses. Their response to and regard for employees depend on the bosses' answers to the question, "What did *you* do for *me* today?"

It does not work. With unusual consistency, decades of research show that respect, not regulation, and empathic concern, not cold calculation, are bosses' most practical tools. Recently, for example, a series of studies on time theft (i.e., the discrepancy between self-recorded punch-out times and the actual times of departure from work) showed that the best empirical predictors of workers' time theft were their supervisors' expressions of compassion and the workers' views of management's respect for employees.[5]

Parallel findings come from a 1998 study of labor protests in Hong Kong. Here, investigators obtained data showing that support for labor protests was greater when on-lookers perceived that management was treating employees "insincerely" and, as if they were simply profit-making machines.[6] One of the most remarkable findings of support for the benefits of bosses' respect and empathic concern comes from an investigation of errors made by airplane cockpit crews. Crews led by warm, friendly pilots made the fewest errors, while those headed by hostile, dictatorial pilots made the most. Evidently, even when employees' work performance affects their physical welfare, it is itself affected by bosses' messages of inclusion and exclusion.[7]

Trust is not merely a social nicety, nor is bosses' caring and concern for employees. Of course, employees are inclined to regard bosses who genuinely have these qualities as "good people." But the value of these bosses to firms goes beyond public relations. By building employees' organizational identity, these bosses are giving their firms a competitive edge with measurable, bottom-line consequences.

Unfortunately, because of current business trends, pressure on bosses to micromanage and sport a coldly calculating, *it-is-all-business* supervisory style endangers their acquisition of this valuable edge.

Micromanaging

In the mid-1990s, a *Harvard Business Review* article described how 3M surpassed one of its competitors, the Norton Company, despite Norton's pioneering use of computer-driven business models to regulate managers' decisions about allocation of assets, varying cash flows, and areas of comparative competitive strength.[8] 3M's successful competition with Norton can be attributed to its core management philosophy, which places emphasis on building trust through actions that release, rather than regulate, employee initiative.

3M's CEO, Livio D. DeSimone, described the company's approach by stating that, "Senior management's primary role is to create an internal environment in which people understand and value our way of operating.... Our job is one of creation and destruction—supporting individual initiative while breaking down bureaucracy and cynicism. It all depends on developing a personal trust relationship between those at the top and those at lower levels."

Similar implications about the practical effects of trust—or its absence—on work performance are evident in the experiences of Westinghouse Electric Corporation. As one commentator reflected, "... by the end of the 1980s, Paul Lego, then president of Westinghouse Electric Corporation, was boasting to *Fortune* that the company had 'the most sophisticated strategic-planning system in the U.S. ... allowing us to portfolio-plan on a micro basis.'"9 Very shortly afterward, events obviously related to those tight regulatory controls betrayed the promise of this "sophisticated strategic-planning system." Reports disclose that Westinghouse Electric Company employees "soon began to spend much of their time simply justifying their units' survival. They stretched projections, inflated estimates, and disguised data."10

The lesson is clear. Shortsighted use of control systems by companies like Norton and Westinghouse endorse and encourage micromanagment. Since all surveillance is ultimately imperfect, monitoring pressures on employees tilt them toward disguising, not disclosing, and on fabricating business-correct facades instead of fixing real problems. At Westinghouse Electric Corporation, the use of these regulatory controls reportedly contributed to write-offs amounting to $5 billion.

When Gordon Bethune became Continental Airlines' CEO in 1994, the company's dismal condition had travelers predicting that its days were numbered. Four years later, its stock price was up 1,700 percent. Lowering micromanagement's restraints on employees, not raising them, was a major reason for Mr. Bethune's success.

"These employees didn't trust us, and after the previous decade it was hard to blame them for that," he said. "Under Frank Lorenzo and other previous CEOs," Bethune continued, "everybody was screwing everybody—no wonder planes were late and the luggage was lost."11 In order to solve Continental's problems, Mr. Bethune might have chosen to set goals, monitor performance, take names, and break heads. He didn't. Instead, he offered employees a deal and gave them freedom to decide how to take advantage of it. Bethune's solution combined sound business objectives with recognition of trust's role in building ties that lead to workforce commitment and initiative.

Bethune offered each employee an extra $65 per month if Continental's index of on-time performance became one of the industry's top five. With 40,000 employees on Continental's payroll, the potential cash cost of moving into the top five was a monthly outlay of $2.6 million, meaning that Continental stood to *gain* $2.4 million per month since late arriving flights were costing the company $5 million per month.

In 1996, the company's on-time performance was among the industry's top five and a new deal was offered: Each employee could receive an additional $100 per month if the on-time index moved into the top three. In addition, Bethune decreased organizational regulation of worker behavior by getting rid of the old manual. He said, "Under the old style of management, symbolized by that authoritarian manual, employees were limited on every side." Constraints on employees were so great that even in unusual customer situations, they were forbidden the freedom to exercise discretion. Bethune reversed all that. Shifting to a set of flexible guidelines, he emphasized goals, not restrictions, and he rewarded task accomplishment instead of punishing rule violation. "We don't want robots," proclaimed Bethune, "we want team members."

Some of Continental's bosses evidently preferred micromanagement and the *we/they* distinctions that it breeds over the changes that Bethune was attempting. They voiced their fears about giving employees greater discretion. But Bethune did not yield. "... 5 percent or so will run wild, take advantage, screw this up" he said, "but the other 95 percent are people who probably will be so glad for the opportunity to do their jobs that they'll easily manage the balancing act between the good of the airline and the good of the customer."

Bethune's success in building employees' organizational identity was illustrated on one occasion when he boarded a Continental Airlines flight and paused to chat with an attendant. Not recognizing him, the gate agent told him to take a seat because the flight had to leave. Quickly, a flight attendant told the agent that he was speaking to CEO Bethune. "That's nice," said the agent, "but we gotta go. Tell him to sit down."

Bethune treated employees respectfully, with trust, indicating their common membership in *we*. By removing pressure on bosses to micro-manage, he raised employees' emotional attachment to the company. Increasing micromanagement would have had the opposite consequence. It tells the "micromanaged" that they are mistrusted, a part of *they* whose potential misbehavior must be prevented through control. Regardless of the content, every effort to regulate work behavior communicates that *they* (employees) are different from and less trustworthy than the bosses who decided that there was a need to closely control *their* behavior.

Rule manuals and sophisticated strategic-planning systems are not the only means used by bosses to micromanage employees' work behavior. In the United States, millions of workers are daily subjected to electronic surveillance.[12] Some of this monitoring is used to diagnose work performance in the service of improving employees' skills. When monitoring is employed for this purpose, its praiseworthy aim is development, not close control. But some of the remaining monitoring is little more than a game of *gotcha*. Its aim is to trap employees by detecting variances and punishing the perpetrators.

Employees who are monitored for purposes of detection show increased stress, decreased satisfaction, and a range of adverse physical symptoms, including eyestrain, headaches, and all sorts of body pains.

These workers are more prone to anxiety, irritability, and depression. Their relationships with peers, supervisors, and bosses are badly degraded. Finally, in an ironic twist, their task performance, which the monitoring is supposed to raise by controlling error, generally declines, regardless of whether the surveillance is electronic or live.[13]

The Boss Club

Why then do some organization authorities persist in their efforts to micromanage workforce behavior? The answer is that it ratifies their status in the *Boss Club*, which boosts their self-concept.

For some, being a boss means that they have been given responsibility for controlling those lower on the hierarchy. It is all about regulation. One of the century's most iconoclastic organization scholars, Massachusetts Institute of Technology's Professor Emeritus Edgar Schein, has observed that bosses often see exercising prerogative as a natural benefit of moving up the organization hierarchy. It is what they have worked for. After all, what is the point of becoming a boss, unless you act like one? Thus, in a twisted way, exercising prerogative establishes bosses' status. It is a behavioral insignia separating bosses from subordinates who lack prerogative—those who were left behind—and, in the act of exercising prerogative, bosses feel joined with an elite to whom they once kowtowed, members of the *Boss Club*.

Few psychological forces in organization life have an impact that compares to those caused by human desire to become part of an elite *we,* and to elevate that group's status (as well as one's own) by regulating *them*. Events in a South African mining company illustrate the power of this force.

Fanagalo is a pidgin language used in South Africa's mines. It uses lots of Zulu words as well as some words that were borrowed from English and Afrikaans. Fanagalo is concerned with regulation. Imperative commands are at the language's core. In fact, "Fanagalo" means "like this," and connotes, "Do it like this." Easily learned, Fanagalo was the solution for white South Africans who wanted to command and control black South Africans coming from different language groups.

Despite a 1996 legislative decision to eliminate Fanagalo, as late as 1998 it was still widely used in the mines. One mine supervisor, a white man, was displeased at production snafus. He summoned the person in charge, a black man, in order to discuss the matter. After arriving at the boss' office, the young black man began explaining, in English, why the problems were occurring. His boss erupted. "What's with the English, eh? Are you trying to be cheeky? Fanagalo has always been good enough for you before. You speak to me in Fanagalo."[14]

English would have been sufficient to get the job done, if the only things at stake were the production snafus. But they were not the only things at stake. In this boss-subordinate encounter, as in so many organization encounters, the other text was the participants' relative status. Fanagalo says something about who is in control. This pidgin language, as well as the regulatory methods used for *gotcha*-oriented electronic surveillance, and by Norton, Westinghouse Electric Corporation, and Continental Airlines in pre-Bethune days, provides controlling bosses with a means of elevating themselves at the expense of employees who are being controlled. Exercising control is an uplifting jolt to many bosses' self-regard. Although, in the long-term, the exclusionary messages sent by these bosses adversely affects workers' organization ties, well-being, and task performance, its short-term pleasures seem an irresistible attraction for too many bosses.

It-Is-All-Business

During the Vietnam conflict, reports discussed *body counts*, not the number of human beings killed. Menus in upscale restaurants offer patrons *sweetbreads*, not cattle glands. Organizations *downsize, right size, deselect, let go*, and *outplace*. They have *premature retirement, redeployment*, and *reorganization*. Their public relations offices release news of *RIFs* (reductions-in-force), *SMAs* (skill-mix-adjustments), and *WICs* (work force-imbalance-corrections). Organizations don't announce that they are *firing workers by the hundreds, or thousands— wives, husbands, daughters, sons, sisters, and brothers whose work and wages are essential to their families' well-being.*

Organizations' announcements of firings are sanitized to the point of being devoid of any human cause or consequence. (By one count, at least four dozen of these vacuous euphemisms are in regular use.[15]) These carefully crafted explanations cast an image of bosses who are objective, matter-of-fact, and exclusively concerned with righting a wrong bottom line. They portray authorities who appear untroubled by their decisions to sacrifice employees for the organization's good; to these bosses, *it-is-all-business.*

Bosses who fire their employees should be troubled by this depiction of themselves. Every piece of credible empirical evidence tells us that when workers are threatened with firing, supportive, empathic (not to be read as either *acquiescent* or *soft-hearted.)* bosses have a more positive effect on their performance and commitment than cool, dispassionate ones do.

Journalism's concern about the rate at which workers were being fired went into high gear in February and March 1996, when *Newsweek's* "Corporate Killers" cover story was quickly followed by the *New York Times'* seven-part report, "The Downsizing of America." Although organization critics and apologists alike responded to these articles through lenses ground by their own biases, neither group fully recognized that the *how* of firings affected survivors' work behavior and society's support for business institutions as much as, and in some instances perhaps more than, the fact that firings were occurring.

Organization critics applauded the news accounts claiming, "I told you so," asking for an end to "corporate greed"—their take on the crisis's major cause. Organization apologists, on the other hand, scurried to find facts supporting their view that the firings were part of an essential, normal, healthy restructuring of the economy.

Critics attacked. Supported by evidence collected by investigators such as Right Associates, they showed that, contrary to apologists' assertions, firing was often used as a first, not a last resort. They presented data proving that 80 percent of companies that fired employees actually were profitable in the year that the dismissals occurred, and companies posting record profits also regularly fired employees. Critics raised doubt about the efficacy of firing as a solution to organization ills by demonstrating that job cuts were ordinarily not one-time events. Indeed, their statistics indicated that the best predictor of whether an organization will be firing employees next year is whether they did so this year: Two-thirds of those that do it in Year One do it again in Year Two.[16]

The failure of firing as a strategy, said the critics, is partly attributable to the costs that organizations bear when they get rid of workers. Immediate, tangible costs to organizations that fire employees include severance payments, outplacement expenses, and expenditures for recruitment (including selection and training). In the slightly longer term, there are also hard-to-measure costs, possibly even higher than the tangible ones, caused by declines in survivors' work performance.

Severance costs vary, but reasonable approximations are a week of severance pay for each year of previous employment given to employees at the lowest levels; eight months' pay given to lower-level executives;

a year's pay to higher-level ones, and the equivalent of three years' income to CEOs. Outplacement costs for professionals and executives range between 10 percent and 15 percent of their annual salary, while recruitment, selection, and training costs are about one-third of their year's salary. Measurable survivor costs for stress after layoffs occur in the form of disability payments, amounting to an average of nearly $2,000 *per employee*.[17] Of course, these figures do not include hidden costs caused by work inefficiencies that begin in the pre-layoff rumor days and continue long after the last employee is fired.

The critics' position was that, because of costs like these, firings not only often fail to produce promised long-term cost savings, they also frequently cause cost increases, as well as more bureaucracy, workplace divisiveness, and customer dissatisfaction.[18] Supporting this conclusion is a major study of 25 firms over seven years. These firms, which fired an average of 31 percent of their workers, were compared to 91 other firms from the same industries that made no such cuts during exactly the same time periods.[19]

In the year before the firings occurred, both the 25 that were going to fire employees and the 91 that weren't experienced sharp earnings declines. In fact, the decline was almost 89 percent for the 91, but only 75 percent for the 25 that eventually got rid of workers. (These differences counter-indicate an alternative contention that those that fired employees did so because they were initially in worse shape than the comparison companies. In fact, in so far as earning declines are concerned, the firms that fired workers were in slightly better shape before the cuts.)

Three years later, earnings of the companies that avoided firing workers rebounded 423 percent, while those that chose a downsizing strategy realized an earnings increase of only 183 percent. Stockholder returns followed the same pattern: After three years, an investment of one dollar in the companies that elected to fire employees earned about five cents. The same dollar invested in companies that did not cut workers earned about seven times more, approximately 35 cents.

Three other studies confirmed these findings, bringing comfort to job cutback critics. One, conducted by the Wyatt Company between 1989 and 1994, showed that profits increased in about 50 percent of the companies using firing as a cost-cutting strategy, but they actually declined in 20 percent of them.[20] A second study, conducted by the American Management Association, revealed that after cuts, only 34 percent of companies reported increases in productivity and, fewer than half, 45 percent, reported improvements in operating profits, but 80 percent said that morale was harmed. The third and final study, undertaken by the Center for Economic

Studies of the Census Bureau, involved a 10-year investigation of 140,000 plants. It provided critics with powerful ammunition for arguing that upsizing, not downsizing, might be the better path toward productivity.

Considering only plants that were regarded as successful upsizers or downsizers, this investigation showed that upsizers' growth in value-added was approximately three times that of downsizers'. That premium to an upsizing strategy occurred despite evidence that labor productivity growth in downsizing plants was 2 percent to 3 percent above that of upsizers. Evidently, fewer employees, with more work piled on each of them, boosted the individual productivity of downsized companies, but not their overall value-added.[21]

A specific example of the benefits of not firing workers occurred in 1994 when United Air Lines (UAL) promised not to lay off unionized pilots and machinists, and then spread the umbrella of protection to salaried workers. Subsequently, reports maintain that turnover in some UAL job categories was down by 50 percent, worker compensation costs fell 26 percent, and absenteeism dropped 10 percent, resulting in an annual savings of between $25 and $30 million.[22]

Apologists retorted. "The critics," they said, "simply do not appreciate the ways in which technological change and global competition demand workplace adjustments." Robert J. Eaton, CEO of Chrysler Corporation, for example, objected to the criticism saying, "Downsizing and layoffs are part of the price of becoming more competitive." "If it did not happen," he added, "the price would be higher."[23] Therefore, unavoidable current pains are insuring future gains in wealth and jobs. Wall Street's response to the firings provides proof of this pain/gain prognosis. Organizations that drive costs down get favorable investor response. For example, when AT&T announced plans to control costs by dismissing 40,000 people, its market value temporarily increased by $4 billion. That means the wealth of stockholders around the world increased by $4,000 million. Thus, say the apologists, by firing people, CEOs are protecting, even growing, the shareholder wealth.

Critics who lament these necessary adjustments, say apologists, are also overlooking the way in which the cost-saving changes are fueling job creation. For example, there was lots of hands wringing in 1996, when AT&T announced its cuts, but not a lot of hands applauding between 1992 and 1996 when 408,000 jobs were created in communication and computer service industries. Nor did many applaud the record numbers of new jobs that the United States economy created for so many years during the 1990s.

New York Times business columnist Louis Uchitelle identified one reason for the hand-wringing/applause discrepancy. He observed that despite both strong job growth and low unemployment rates, layoffs in the 1990s were ahead of 1980 levels.[24] Layoffs are measured by job loss rate, not levels of unemployment or re-employment. Sometimes called *displacement*, this neglected index is equal to the number of people losing their jobs as a percentage of the labor force. Displacement rate is a barometer of threat. It has a great deal to do with employees' feelings of fright, security, expendability, and exclusion.

After the economic recession of the early 1990s ended, for the rest of the decade the percent of the labor force claiming that they had lost jobs involuntarily hovered around 8 percent.[25] This is an important number for two reasons: First, by historical standards, it is a relatively high figure. Second, the statistic's year-to-year consistency means that the absolute number of people being fired from their jobs was actually increasing, even as unemployment rates declined, since the size of the work force was increasing.

The Issue Is Displacement, Not Unemployment, Stupid!

Employees' attachment to current employers erodes as the threat of being fired by them grows. The probability of landing new jobs is a psychologically remote statistic that might raise or lower anxiety about the aftermath of being fired, but it has little effect on workers' feelings about today's threatening bosses. From this perspective, recent patterns of displacement following recession are ominously different from the pattern that occurred in the early 1980s. Then, in the five-year period after the recession ended, the rate of displacement fell to 6.5 percent from 9 percent. By the mid-1990s, because of the unflagging 8 percent rate of displacement, 75 percent of U.S. families reported suffering a relative's, friend's, or neighbor's job loss. Surveys showed that one out of every two adults worried that one or more household members would lose their jobs within three years. And nearly three-fourths of those surveyed confessed to believing that job loss was a permanent feature of the U.S. labor market. [26]

Those beliefs must have been reinforced at the end of the millennium when U.S. companies announced their layoff plans. The numbers were the decade's highest. In 1998, companies warned that they were planning 678,000 layoffs. In the following year, 1999, they promised an additional 675,000. The actual numbers were much higher. Data collected by the

Bureau of Labor Statistics, which includes layoffs that occur but are not announced, indicate that approximately 1.6 million workers were fired from their jobs in 1999.[27] This trend continued right into the first years of the new millennium as business leaders responded to a declining economy by cutting both costs and personnel.

These data make it clear that worry about job loss, not confidence about re-employment, is a constant companion to most workers and their families. Job availability in the surrounding market simply is not a cure for job loss concerns. It is difficult to have familiar daily patterns of waking, traveling, shopping, and friends wrenched away.[28] Job loss requires facing uncertainty, potentially lower salary (about two-thirds of the time), and feelings of humiliation. Children might ask difficult questions, spouses might grieve, and too few resources might remain available in order to take care of aging parents, school tuition, infant day care, or an occasional movie. Apologists who point to low unemployment rates arguing, *There are lots of jobs about. Why worry?* are focusing on the smoothed trend lines of aggregated statistics, conveniently forgetting that those lines mask jagged peaks and valleys of individual experience.

In 1998, when Xerox announced plans to cut 10 percent of its 91,400 employees, Jonathan Rosenzweig, a Salomon Smith Barney analyst, was quoted as asking, "What can be wrong about a message that entails, on top of accelerating top-line growth, the ability to cut cost from a position of strength and further boost the bottom line?"[29] The answer is, "Nothing's wrong, if they do it right."

Firings are inevitable. They are sometimes also a necessary response to changes in markets and technology that no one could have anticipated. The question is not whether they *will* occur (they will), nor whether they *should* occur (sometimes they should). Rather, it is *how* they will be conducted. Bosses' empathic concern is disabled when they focus on probabilities and profits over people. From employees' perspective, when these bosses fire their workmates, the bosses' behavior is no more than a product of cold calculation—*it-is-all-business*. These bosses seem to be roaming organizational corridors arbitrarily hunting for targets of opportunity. Their conscious preoccupation appears to be with constraints caused by legal procedures, politics, and public relations, and finding methods for getting around them. Hours of discussion seem to be about constructing ways of denying leaks, keeping secrecy, and releasing information only when it prevents *them* (employees) from creating trouble for *us* (bosses). The message from bosses to employees reads, *You're expendable.* It is a message of exclusion.

Firings often cause employees to feel doubly dismissed. The first dismissal occurs when they or their colleagues lose jobs. The second dismissal is of them as human beings, who also happen to be employees. The two dismissals occur simultaneously when the firing happens without any evidence that bosses understand, much less care about, what the experience of being fired means to its victims. *In taking these regrettable actions*, their bosses' communiques say, *we will abide by every applicable organization and government regulation*, with the unwritten addition being, *Beyond that your needs in this matter are not our concern.*

When it comes to the *how* of firing, actions speak at least as loud as words: At Kodak, on one occasion, dismissal slips were simply added to employees' pay envelopes without any warning. In another company, a father was fired in front of his eight-year-old daughter on "Take Your Daughter to Work" day. At Allied Bank of Texas, the names of employees being fired were publicly announced at a meeting called for this special purpose.[30] CPC Specialty Foods, located in the Bronx, New York, manufactures Melba Toast. On an April morning in 1997, when its 200 employees showed up for work they found a list, posted to a wall, containing the names of 45 workers who were fired. Many of the 200 had been CPC employees for two and three decades. As one of the former employees said, "No warning, nothing."[31]

In 1997, Robert S. (Steve) Miller, a specialist in organization turn-arounds, was a director and acting CEO of Waste Management, Inc. Part of his responsibility as acting CEO was to find a permanent replacement for himself. In the course of working on that task he announced to the company's 58,000-person workforce, "I wouldn't support a Chainsaw Al. This (*Author's note:* Waste Management, Inc.) is a great asset. We're not going to rip the place apart and destroy things."[32] "Chainsaw Al" is Albert Dunlap, an organization turnaround specialist whose nickname says it all: His approach to fixing organizations possesses the empathy of someone committing the Texas Chainsaw Massacre. By referring to "*a* Chainsaw Al" not *the* Chainsaw Al, however, CEO Steve Miller was recognizing that when it comes to *organization chain sawing*, Mr. Dunlap has lots of company. Other bosses might not have his capacity for newsworthy sound bites, but their actions reveal kinship with Mr. Dunlap's orientation to *how* firings are conducted and the message of exclusion that it conveys.

One report of Mr. Dunlap's history begins at Lily-Tulip Company where, between 1983 and 1986, he cut headquarters personnel 50 percent and salaried workers 20 percent. During the next three years, at Crown-Zellerbach, he cut staff 22 percent and reduced distribution centers from 22 to 4. In 1989, at Australian National Industries he engineered a 47 percent cut in personnel. Then he went on to fire 11,200 employees at Scott Paper, about 31 percent of the workforce. After Scott Paper, Mr. Dunlap signed on at Sunbeam Corporation where he fired approximately 50 percent of the workforce.[33]

Employees' understanding of the *how* of Albert Dunlap's chain-saw strategy is based on more than merely the number of people he has fired. Talking to a reporter on one occasion, Mr. Dunlap revealed things that certainly say a lot about his orientation to organizations and their employees: "I like predators," he admitted, "I like them because they live by their wits."[34] The analogy, or some variation of it, so commonly used by organization authorities, is dangerous to organizational health. It has two problems. First, it gives too much credit to predators and not enough to their prey. Both live by their wits, which frequently cause predators to lose more prey than they catch. In the case of lions, for example, perhaps 1 in 12 attacks results in a kill. Second, the analogy is dangerously misleading. Relationships in organizations are portrayed as if they were the same as those that exist in the wild between predators and prey. They are not.

Among subhuman species, predators survive by killing and consuming prey. Successful hunters win at the expense of the hunted. In organizations, individuals might engage in bloodthirsty competition for promotions, and groups might compete for budget, but ultimately, organizational survival requires cooperation, commitment, and teamwork. Further, even if subhuman predators were capable of doing the thinking, they could not afford to have empathy for their prey's circumstances; its inhibiting effects on strangling, slashing, and gnawing would hamper their survival. Thus, bosses like Albert Dunlap who see the world through empathy-free, predator/prey lenses might be sending their workforces the ultimate in *us/them* messages.

Events at Biddeford Textile Company, located at the falls of the Saco River in Biddeford, Maine, also say a great deal about the *how* of Dunlap-style organization chain sawing. In 1996 the company's 352 employees produced and shipped approximately four million shells for electric blankets. In fact, before 1996, if you bought an electric blanket produced in the United States, its shell was probably made at Biddeford. Sunbeam Corporation owned the company.

Employees at Biddeford Textile who felt secure because of the firm's production and sales history probably received a wake-up call in November 1996 when CEO Dunlap announced that the plant was to be sold or shut down. The United States Secretary of Labor said that Dunlap's plan was "treating the employees as if they were disposable pieces of equipment." Mr. Dunlap reportedly dismissed the comment. His job was to make profits for the stockholders.

Two days before Christmas, 37 Biddeford Textile employees, about 10 percent of the company's workforce, were fired.[35] Even if Sunbeam's stockholders preferred firing as a strategy, it is hard to believe that they also wanted (or were financially served by) this organization chain sawing 48 hours before Christmas Day.

A Biddeford Textile employee said, "Family traditions—that means this much (*showing a zero with his fingers*) to Al Dunlap." Another added, "Chainsaw Al doesn't care who he steps on and squashes, as long as he gets paid his millions." As he did with the Secretary of Labor's comment, Mr. Dunlap reportedly treated these characterizations of him as misguided. "Everyone whose job is threatened sees me as the villain because I am the visible symbol of change." He's exaggerating. His visibility as an agent of organization change was only part of the reason why employees feel they were victims of organizational villainy. If the world's Dunlaps wonder why workers boo rather than applaud their organizational rescue efforts, it is because *the way* they do what they do appears riddled with a lack of empathy and respect for members of the workforce.

Sunbeam Corporation eventually became Mr. Dunlap's Waterloo. In July 1996, when he joined the company, Sunbeam's stock price hovered at $12.50. After rising 49 percent on the day that his appointment was announced, over the next two years it climbed to a high of $53. Then, in June 1998, only three months after reaching that price peak, the stock tumbled to $25 per share.[36] There was bad news.

Selling barbecue grills to major customers, like Kmart Corporation, for huge discounts, allegedly bolstered 1997 end-of-year figures. The ripple effects of these inducements were manifest in early 1998's terrible results. There were complaints: "Mr. Dunlap succeeded in slashing costs at Sunbeam, eliminating 12,000 jobs. But he wasn't able to deliver on his promise to transform the company into a high-growth profit machine..."[37] and there were questions: Had organization chain sawing strengthened the company as a productive enterprise? Was there any long-term development in product manufacturing and distribution, or were all the changes short-term financial ones? Did the changes in stock price give the company room to maneuver as an acquisition and divestiture player with no, or possibly adverse, effects on its capacity as a producer?

As if in answer to some of these questions, when Albert Dunlap was fired from his job as Sunbeam's CEO, instead of shedding tears, Joseph Taylor, who was a manager at Sunbeam's Coushette, Louisiana plant for

16 years said, "I guess the house of cards came tumbling down.... When you reduce your workforce by 50 percent, you lose your ability to manage. You can survive like that for months, but not years."[38] Someone "familiar with the situation" supported Mr. Taylor's conclusion. He disclosed that the board "had lost confidence in Al Dunlap's ability to carry out the long-term growth potential of the company."[39]

Although the final chapters of this story are still being written, on Friday, January 11, 2002, without admitting any wrongdoing, a number of former Sunbeam Corporation executives, including Mr. Dunlap, agreed to settle a stockholders' lawsuit by paying $15 million to them. There was a second settlement with bondholders and investors, but its terms were not made public.[40]

Sacrificing *Them*

Sunbeam's decision to fire Mr. Dunlap raises important questions about who should be "paying the piper" for an organization's mistakes. These questions are important because if some members of an organization unilaterally exclude themselves from paying, it marks them as members of an elite in-group and, simultaneously, condemns those they designate as "payers" to membership in an expendable out-group.

Albert Dunlap neither needs or deserves defenders, but someone must ask whether he alone deserved punishment. Even if his competence was judged fairly and found wanting, was his firing also a public sacrifice that distracted attention from other, equally culpable organization authorities? Al Dunlap did precious little as Sunbeam's CEO that could not have been predicted in advance. If his chain-saw approach to Sunbeam's rescue did not work, there is *prima facie* evidence that the error of judging what remedy to introduce was the board's as well as his. Maybe Albert Dunlap had to be replaced by someone with different skills, but should the board that appointed him in the first place be exempt from penalty?

After errors occur in organizations, pain might be a necessary prerequisite to gain. The central question is, how will the burden of pain be distributed? In organizations, it seems that self-serving decisions by those standing on the hierarchies' upper rungs disproportionately displace the burden of pain onto those standing beneath them. Boards do it to CEOs. CEOs do it to managers. Managers do it to supervisors. And so it goes, right down the ladder, until employees, completely innocent of any involvement in costly decisions, are forced to bear the burden of the incompetence of those standing above them.

At Mutual America's annual employees' meeting, Bill Flynn, the company's chairman, is reported to have said, "If the company ever had to institute a corporation layoff policy, it would not be because someone in the mailroom had made a mistake." The mistake would be his, he admitted, promising to put his name at the top of the list of those being fired.[41] Mr. Flynn's willingness to take the blame for the pain is atypical.

In 1986, AT&T fired 32,000 employees in order to streamline. In 1988, another 16,000 were fired because modernization created job obsolescence. Then, 14,000 more were fired in 1991 as part of a unit phaseout in order to make way for an acquisition. Streamlining was again the reason given for 15,000 firings in 1994, 8,500 in 1995, and 40,000 in 1996. The day AT&T announced its plans to fire 40,000 workers in 1996, its stock price rose approximately 4 percent. This, despite the fact that insiders were quoted as acknowledging that the cuts were a morale-devastating means of undoing the consequences of wrong decisions made by managers who were still on the job.[42] They claimed that management, under CEO Robert Allen, "blew upward of $12 billion on losses and acquisitions."

Allen responded, "If everything we did was absolutely perfect or correct, maybe we'd be given another name and be called God or something. So, things did not work out. We move on to something else." *We*, in this case, could not have included approximately 100,000 ATT employees who had been fired from their jobs. *They* had no part in the costly management decisions, but *they* were forced to sacrifice their jobs in order to undo the decisions' costly consequences. Organizations grow portly because of management errors. Regardless of whether these errors are caused by management's stupid use of facts or their seduction by market forces, it is hard to understand why the pain of remedy falls so heavily on employees who simply did the work that they were asked to do.

"The noisiest skeleton rattling around at AT&T is the computer business. First, AT&T tried unsuccessfully to build a computer operation internally. Then, in 1991, it grabbed NCR, paying $7.5 billion for a business at that time making around $350 million."[43] By 1995, AT&T managed the business to a loss of $600 million on top of a $1.6 billion charge that was incurred when it moved out of PC manufacturing.

The computer business might have been the noisiest skeleton that AT&T management put into the closet, but the NCR fiasco was only one of its rattling bones. AT&T also bought the Imagination Network, a company that offered games over the Internet. In a year that America Online added 3,000,000 subscribers, the AT&T purchase reportedly netted a total of 62,000 new subscribers. Costs were also incurred when AT&T tried to enter e-mail service by purchasing Easylink (renamed Personlink) and making investments in technology developed by General Magic Inc. Eventually, these purchases were alleged to be the cause of a $1.1 billion pretax charge against earnings.[44] Jobs had to be sacrificed in order to off-set these losses.

Sacrificing innocent employees can be painful. Menninger Clinic mental health professionals have a long history helping bosses manage the psychological disturbance they experience after firing subordinates.[45] It is evident that for some bosses the disturbance occurs because they empathetically know employees' pain. On their command, faithful, earnest workers who ought to be rewarded for their efforts have been dismissed instead.

For other bosses, Menninger's professional ministrations appear irrelevant. An *it-is-all-business* attitude of indifference protects these bosses from the pain that's caused when they sacrifice innocent employees. Sacrificing one of *them* never produces as much pain as sacrificing one of *us*. Seeing employees as *them* disengages the psychological golden rule of organizations (*Harming you becomes difficult for me because the two of us are part of* we) by obstructing empathy. The victims are not Joe and Joanna, wage-earning husband, wife, son, or daughter. They are *depersonalized* into indistinguishable parts of a RIF (reduction-in-force), SMA (skill-mix-adjustment), or WIC (work force-imbalance-correction). And, they are *scapegoats* who deserve punishment because their "job inadequacies" are harming the firm, or because they are necessary *sacrifices* for the greater good that is at stake.

With All Due Respect

Jerry W. Levin was Mr. Dunlap's replacement at Sunbeam. According to reports, during his first day on the job Mr. Levin separated himself and his new culture from Mr. Dunlap and his culture by announcing that "tough guy talk, top-down management, and bragging in advance of profit" were not the thing to do. Sending a clear message of inclusion, Mr. Levin continued by assuring employees that "he would listen to their views on market potential rather than dictating sales objectives" and added, "I have made bigger mistakes in my career than all of you put together."[46]

Wall Street liked what it heard. On the day of those announcements, Sunbeam's shares rose about 15 percent. Obviously, remedy does not require an *it-is-all-business* orientation.

It is business, but it is not *all* business. Certainly, successful remedy requires correct construction of the *what* of work, including such things as finances, technology, product design, and the chronology and course of various strategic plans. But if the *how* of implementation is incorrectly constructed, it might very well nullify every bit of wisdom that the *what* contains.

Levi Strauss, the clothing manufacturer known for its denim, understands there is a need to attend to both. Despite sales of $7.1 billion, in 1996, the company lost market share to competitors such as Guess, Gitano, and to private brands like J C Penney's Arizona jeans. As a consequence, in November 1997, the company announced plans to curtail costs by cutting manufacturing jobs in the United States by one-third. For this progressive company, the decision to fire employees was unusual. But the business plan's contents as well as the process of planning for the dismissals, including participation of the Union of Needletrades, Industrial and Textile Employees (UNITE), helped to create remedy while simultaneously preserving Levi Strauss as an organization that includes its workforce inside the firm's *we*-group boundary.

Bruce Raynor, UNITE's executive vice president, described Levi Strauss' plan as "by far the best severance settlement apparel workers have ever gotten."[47] By offering workers a package that met their legitimate needs, not simply government's minimum legal requirements, Levi Strauss gave them the platform they needed in order to find alternative employment. Pay continued for eight months, although work responsibility stopped. Workers received three weeks' salary for every year that they worked at Levi Strauss, their health benefits were continued for 18 months, $6,000 was available to them for education, training, or moving, and those who found new jobs were eligible for $500 bonuses. Finally, $8 million was available to harmed communities.

Greg Shank, Levi Strauss' president, is quoted as saying, "We're doing this because we believe it is the right thing to do for our employees… (They) have served us for a long time and this decision is not because of them." He added, they need "an appropriate level of support."[48]

After the September 11, 2002 terrorist attack on the World Trade Center Towers, New York City's economy declined and its unemployment rates grew. Two New York businesses, Maurice Villency, a furniture chain, and Patricia Tanaka and Company, a public relations firm, were among a large number of companies that suffered losses in revenues. But these two parted company with many of the other victims by promising not to use dismissal as a first response to their problems. Ms. Tanaka, head of the firm that carries her name, said that "consistency is a business advantage. Clients prefer staying in contact with the same employees." Eric Villency added that in his company, "firing people would be like committing suicide." In fact, both companies have higher retention rates than their respective industries' averages. Norman Tenenbaum, a Maurice Villency employee, explained why: "I stay loyal because the company has been loyal to me."[49]

Economically sensible business decisions that violate employees' expectations about the respect that they are due can ignite responses in them that incinerate bosses' projections of profit. When their plans go up in smoke, it is silly for bosses to lament, "The business decision was right. It's *their* attitude and behavior that's wrong." Bosses' coldly calculating it-is-all-business view of work might have gotten the *what* right while completely destroying the *how* by communicating disrespectful messages of exclusion that heighten employee alienation, fatally affecting their motivation and performance.

Some alleged experts incorrectly believe that these unwelcome outcomes can be avoided by merely managing appearances, regardless of bosses' true intent. *If you're going to fire folks*, they say, *do it at day's end, so that they will cool-off overnight.* "Wear clothing that will make you appear more open...no turtlenecks or pin-stripes.... Avoid sharp lines and geometric tie patterns in favor of round paisleys." Wearing black, they warn, is especially inadvisable.[50]

Interviews that I conducted with workers who had been fired made me realize how quickly they see through this type of manipulation. Once it becomes transparent, such trickery not only stops working, it boomerangs. Its implicit message, they *are dumb enough to be fooled by us all of the time*, produces alienation and anger. Of course, no matter how cleverly the *how* is constructed, firing will never be fun. Nonetheless, respectful messages of inclusion, like those sent by Levi Strauss' plan, tend to have more favorable individual and organization consequences than disrespectful messages of exclusion do.

Boss behavior almost always contains information about the organization's regard for employees. Because of employees' heightened vigilance, this is especially true during times of crisis. But three areas of boss behavior are particularly crucial determinants of workers' views about the respect that they are receiving from employers, their subsequent ties to them, and their work commitment. The first area is communication: Is accurate, timely information being shared, or are *they* trying to deceive *us*?

Organization support, especially activities related to workforce training and education, is the second area of behavior that employees scrutinize for clues about their bosses' regard for them. Workers wonder, "is anyone preparing us to deal with the impact of troubling organization circumstances, or are *we* being jettisoned by *them* to sink or swim on our own?"

Finally, bosses' explorations of remedies for organizational problems is the third area in which workers find clues about their employer's regard for them: Are remedies being sought that distribute the pain, or is the selfishness quotient so high that *we* take the pain in order for *them* to enjoy the gain?

Communication

When firing is planned, *includobosses* speak to the workforce about why it will happen and how it will happen, early and often. Using secrets, stealth, and surprise, the *excludobosses'* way, feeds negative emotions, rumor, and behavior that are harmful to both organizations and their employees. (Warning employees of impending layoffs also has financial benefit for communities. Early notification has cut unemployment time by as much as 25 percent, leading to hundreds of millions of dollars in savings for communities that are able to curtail unemployment costs by timely creation of responses such as job programs.[51]) Survivors of firings who believe that timely company communications contain genuine concern, display more organization commitment than surviving employees who believe that their company's communications are scant and uncaring.[52]

Fortuitously, six weeks before one company made a decision to lay off some of its assembly plant workers, a number of them who were already participating in research had prepared written descriptions of what it was like to work for their company. At the researcher's initiative, the company's announcements of the layoffs at different locations were systematically varied. Some announcements of the impending dismissals were filled with information and concern, but others were not. Immediately after the announcements occurred, descriptions of what it was like to work for the company were written again. The results: No differences in favorableness toward the company existed six weeks before the layoffs were announced. But after the decision became public, workers exposed to messages communicating information and concern were far less negative in their descriptions of the company than those receiving the it-is-all-business type announcements.[53]

In another case, a manufacturing firm producing small-machined parts for automotive and aerospace customers suffered a loss of revenue because of a contract cancellation. Rather than lay off employees, the firm decided to manage its temporary cash flow problem by reducing pay in the two affected plants by 15 percent for a 10-week period. Let's call them Plants A and B. An unaffected third plant, Plant C, was left to run normally. Plant A's employees received an announcement with lots of information explaining the pay reduction's what, why, and how, accompanied by expressions of management's concern about the cut's human consequences. Plant B's employees received an announcement of the cuts along with the information-rich explanation but without any expression of concern. Plant C, the one in which no cuts were to occur, received no announcement at all.

Measures taken 10 weeks before the cuts were announced, when the cuts ended, and 10 weeks after employees returned to pre-cut pay levels showed the benefits of empathic expression. Before the announcement, employee theft and turnover were roughly equal in Plants A, B, and C. The same was true 10 weeks after things returned to pre-cut pay levels. But during the interim, vast differences emerged. Employee theft in Plant B was approximately *double* what it was in Plants A or C. It had increased by about 250 percent. Turnover in Plant B, at 25 percent, was also much greater than that of Plant A, which was 2 percent, or Plant C, which had no turnover at all.

Stealing from an it-is-all-business bureaucracy is easy. So is exiting. *They* excluded *us* therefore *we* exclude *them*. Since there is no attachment between the organization and its employees, no *us*, the psychological golden rule of organizations is inoperative. There is no mental conduit through which *their* loss travels to become a source of discomfort that might inhibit *our* personal desire to gain. Therefore, losses for *them* that yield gains for *us* are simply sensible ways of giving ourselves the best possible deal.

Other scientifically controlled comparisons of workers' responses to negative decisions, including firing, tell us that providing credible accounts of why a decision is the way it is has comparatively favorable effects on acceptance even when the decision's outcome is contrary to employees' preferences. Why? Because bosses' honest admissions of mitigating circumstances, political constraints, and potentially adverse decision outcomes encourage employees to believe that they have been treated with respect.[54] In response, employees tend to express relatively more favorable views of bosses, their decision-making, its outcomes, and the organization.[55] But make no mistake; it is not merely the content of the bosses' accounting that has those beneficial effects. It is also the bosses' act of accounting. Taking time to explain (when the explanation is perceived as genuine, not manipulative[56]) is, *de facto,* an expression of respect. It says to employees that their bosses' regard for them is guided by the psychological golden rule of organizations. Secrecy and deception are used in dealings with *them,* but not in dealings with *us.*

Organization Support—Plans for Training and Education

The advisable alternative to firing is enhanced employability, not guaranteed employment. Providing victims and survivors of downsizing with skills that increase their chances of future employment affirms an organization's commitment to its workforce. On a practical level, in-company training is associated with a 20 percent reduced likelihood of job loss and, if a loss occurs, with a 30 percent reduction in the time that passes before finding a new job.[57] Moreover, in a three-year period, firms introducing formal training programs experienced a 19 percent advantage in productivity increases over those that did not.[58] Despite these benefits, there is evidence that perhaps as many as 89 percent of U.S. employees never receive any formal training.[59] In fact, although 90 percent of executives proclaim that employees are their firms' most precious assets, they rank training at the bottom of their list of priorities.[60]

Given these data, it is not surprising that many firms regularly still use a *dismiss-and-replace* strategy in order to keep pace with change. Employees with obsolescent or overly expensive skills are dismissed. Replacements with the abilities required to meet today's demands are hired. These replacements work until either obsolescence or competitive pricing overtakes them, and then the cycle begins again. The *dismiss-and-replace* strategy treats employees as expendable commodities. It sends them a message of exclusion. Retraining is an alternative that sends a message of inclusion.

When organizations' training and education programs make reasonable efforts to go beyond their own immediate needs by offering educational opportunities that are influenced by longer-term organizational needs as well as by employees' vocational goals and their market potential, those programs are sending employees respectful messages of inclusion. They are saying, *we are concerned about you, not just the product that you delivered to us today.*

NYNEX Corporation made a stab at this more inclusive approach to change when it committed to retraining approximately two-thirds of what was then a 60,000-person workforce. The agreement for this retraining program, developed in collaboration with two unions—the Communication Workers of America (CWA) and the International Brotherhood of Electrical Workers (IBEW)—was heralded by the United States Secretary of Labor as a model for other companies.

Called Next Step, the program gave employees an opportunity to earn an Associate of Applied Sciences degree. NYNEX subsidies included one day off each week to attend classes, tuition, books, a laptop computer, and access to the Internet. The course work was practical, designed to put attendees on the cutting-edge of telecommunications. Assessments were competency based. In addition to the subsidies, NYNEX told employees "this is for real" by rewarding them through promotion and salary just for entering Next Step.

Did employees recognize the program's value and were they willing to do the extra work? An 800 number that was set up as a means through which employees could arrange to take the program's entrance exam immediately received 9,250 calls.[61]

During the early 1990s, Chevron USA employed thousands of employees more than its changed business needs required. As was the case with Levi Strauss, Chevron managed the business crisis by attending to both the *what* and the *how*. Retraining programs prepared employees for positions inside and outside the company. Courses were available on topics ranging from computer technology to job-hunting skills. Financial help was available for those who wanted to upgrade academic credentials. Reportedly, 900 employees deployed to different positions at a savings of $25 million in severance pay.[62] It is impossible to say how much saving also might have occurred because Chevron's efforts caused its employees to mentally move the organization icon further into the *we* side of their *we/they* boundary.

Exploration of Alternatives

When they turn their backs on firing as a first resort, bosses send their employees clear messages of inclusion. By exploring the viability of alternatives, bosses are saying to employees, We *are in this together, sharing the burdens as well as the blessings*. This is a far cry from boss behavior communicating that The Company *is burdened with troubles, but if we sacrifice you, then our blessings can continue.*

Reflexite Corporation, a Connecticut-based business that produces reflecting materials, is one example of a company that showed employees respect by trying to share the burden. During difficult financial times in 1991, Cecil Ursprung, Reflexite's CEO, was advised to cut costs by cutting personnel. He forsook the advice. Instead, top management took a 10 percent cut in pay, lower and middle managers had cuts of 7 percent and 5 percent, respectively, and all other employees were released from work, without pay, for one day each month. As a result of this and other similar measures, no firing occurred and, in 1992, Reflexite received an Entrepreneur-of-the-Year award from *Inc.* magazine.[63]

In 1994, there were reports that a division of Intel used graduated pay cuts to save jobs. There were 10 percent cuts for the division's highest paid employees, and none at all for its lowest paid. Similarly, when Volkswagen Europe was in a financial crunch it moved to a 4-day, 29-hour workweek, reportedly saving 30,000 jobs in a 100,000-person workforce.[64] Nucor, the steel producer, also dealt with business reversals by going to a four-day workweek. And, when Deluxe Corporation, a check printing company, had to close 26 of 41 plants, CEO John A. Blanchard III extended the closings so that they occurred over a two-year period. He also raised company funding of education for each worker to $7,500 from $2,000, using efforts in the training and education area to send his workforce the same respectful, inclusive message. [65]

Lincoln Electric Company managed its financial troubles by moving workers into clerical jobs. A&R Welding Inc. created a crew of welders who could attend to the needs of geographically distant customers. And, Apex Precision Technologies continually trains its workers on all of its equipment so that they can shift depending on the composition of each week's orders.[66]

Ken Sweet, general manager of Parker Hannifin's Daedal division, is also a boss who looked for alternatives to dismissal when he faced hard financial times. The division, a single factory with 130 workers, manufactures products that help customers automate their operations. As the economy declined in 2001, Daedal's sales fell 40 percent and pressures mounted on Ken Sweet to cut costs by cutting personnel.

Instead of caving into these pressures, Mr. Sweet got creative. He reorganized employees so that their efforts shifted to hot business possibilities and away from cooling ones. A number of employees worked to develop relations with potential customers. Others joined the busier production groups, making it possible to cut required production times by adding effort. And some employees undertook work that was being outsourced. When the financial crunch became still more severe, compelling payroll adjustment, Mr. Sweet asked employees for their opinions about two alternatives: layoffs and voluntary time off.

The voting that finally occurred showed a split between Daedal's factory and office workers. One out of 10 factory workers preferred voluntary time off, but three out of four office workers had that preference. With Solomon-like wisdom, Mr. Sweet decided that the days off for the two groups would be different: Factory workers would have three to four days of voluntary time off, but office workers would have only two days off. In order to offset that imbalanced burden, however, Mr. Sweet also decided that when it came to raises, factory workers would get priority. Mr. Sweet understands the value of creating *we* as well as the contribution made to it by companies' genuine pursuit of alternatives to dismissal.[67]

Listen hard and you can hear employees' reasoning: *There is no respect when the information being dished out to us is misleading and deceptive. Nor is there any when they wash their hands of any concern with our future, or when they hastily embrace firing as a method for treating business ills.*

Bosses who plan to deal with managing the *how* by suddenly "getting religion," showing respect to employees just when they are about to fire them, are going to be disappointed. The workforce will not read their tardy efforts as genuine respectful messages of inclusion. Employees' emotional attachments to employers are not easily born when their physical links to them are about to die. Attachment is a process that begins building on the day that first contact for hiring occurs. From that time onward, its growth depends on conditions affecting the three Rs of organization life: **R**ewards, **R**espect, and, the one to which we now turn, **R**ecognition.

[1] Ballon, M. "eXtreme." *Inc.* (July 1998): 60–72.

[2] Ibid., 70.

[3] Ibid.

[4] Deogun, N. "Pepsi's Mr. Nice Guy vows not to finish last." *Wall Street Journal* (March 19, 1997): B1, B5.

[5] Greenberg, J. and K. S. Scott. "Why do workers bite the hands that feed them? Employee theft as a social exchange process." *Research in Organizational Behavior* 18 (1996): 111–156.

[6] Leving, K., W-H. Chiu, and Y-F. Au. "Sympathy and support for industrial actions: A justice analysis." *Journal of Applied Psychology* 78 (1993): 781–787.

[7] Hogan, R., G. J. Curphy, and J. Hogan. "What we know about leadership." *American Psychologist* 49 (June 1994): 493–504.; Hackman, J. R. *Leading Teams.* Harvard Business Press, 2002.

[8] Bartlett, C. A. and S. Ghoshal. "Changing the role of top management: Beyond systems to people." *Harvard Business Review* (May–June, 1995): 132–142.

[9] Ibid.

[10] Ibid.

[11] Bethune, G. and S. Huler. "From worst to first." *Fortune* (May 25, 1998): 185–190.

[12] Boyle, M. "Their counting your hours." *Fortune* (March 18, 2002): 184.

[13] Aiello, J. R. "Computer-based work monitoring: Electronic surveillance and its effects." *Journal of Applied Social Psychology* 23 (1993): 499–507; Aiello, J. R. and C. M. Svec. "Computer monitoring of work performance: Extending the social facilitation framework to electronic presence." *Journal of Applied Social Psychology* 23 (1993): 537–548.

[14] Block R. "Just do it: Fanagalo, lingo of apartheid survives in the mines." *Wall Street Journal* (April 15, 1998): A1, A10.

[15] "News in review." *New York Times* (May 26, 1996): 2.

[16] Casio, W. F. "Guide to responsible restructuring." United States Department of Labor. Office of the American Workplace, 1995.

[17] Ibid.

[18] Bennett, A. "Downsizing doesn't necessarily bring an upswing in corporate profitability." *Wall Street Journal* (June 9, 1991): B1, B4; Brockner, J., S. Grover, T. Reed, R. DeWitt, and M. O'Malley. "Survivors' reactions to layoffs: We get by with a little help from our friends." *Administrative Science Quarterly* 32 (1987): 526–554; Burke, W.W. "The agenda for organization development." Presented at the Organization Development Network Annual Conference, Orlando, Florida (October 5, 1996); Casio, W. F. "Downsizing: What do we know? What have we learned?" *Academy of Management Executive* 7 (1993): 95–104; Cole, R. E. "Learning from learning theory: Implications for quality improvements in turnover, use of contingent work, and job rotation policies." *Quality Management Journal* 1 (1993): 9–25; Cameron, K. S., S. J. Freeman and A. K. Mishra. "Best practices in white-collar downsizing: Managing contradictions." *Academy of Management Executive* 5 (1991): 57–73; Henkoff, R. "Getting beyond downsizing." *Fortune* (January 10, 1994): 58–64.

[19] Casio, W. F. "Guide to responsible restructuring." United States Department of Labor. Office of the American Workplace, 1995.

[20] Ibid.

[21] Noble, B. P. "Questioning productivity beliefs." *New York Times* (July 10, 1994): F21.

[22] White, J. B. and J. S. Lublin. "Some companies try to rebuild loyalty." *Wall Street Journal* (September 27, 1996): B1, B6.

[23] Meredith, R. "Executive defends downsizing." *New York Times* (March 19, 1996): D4.

[24] Uchitelle, L. "Muscleman, or 98-pound weakling?" *New York Times* (October 10, 1998): BU1, 11.

25 Stevenson, R. W. "Revised data show layoff rate constant in 1990s." *New York Times* (October 26, 1996): A37–A38.

26 Lohr, S. "Though upbeat on the economy, people still fear for their jobs." *New York Times* (December 29, 1996): A1, A22.

27 Barta, P. "Zero-sum gain." *Wall Street Journal* (March 13, 2000): A1, A16.

28 Shellenbarger, S. "Along with benefits and pay, employees seek friends on the job." *Wall Street Journal* (February 20, 2002): B1.

29 Narisetti, R. "Xerox to cut 9,000 jobs over two years." *Wall Street Journal* (April 8, 1998): A6.

30 Folger, R. and D. P. Skarlicki. "When tough times make tough bosses: Managerial distancing as a function of layoff blame." *Academy of Management Journal* 41 (1998): 79–87.

31 "Layoffs: The personal touch." *New York Times* (April 6, 1997): F2.

32 Bailey, J. and G. Jaffe. "When 'Chainsaw Al' puts pen to paper it can be a massacre." *Wall Street Journal* (December 22, 1997): A1, A8.

33 Frank, R. and J. S. "Lublin Dunlap's ax falls—6,000 times—at Sunbeam." *Wall Street Journal* (November 13, 1996): B1, B12.

34 Collins G. "Tough leader wields the ax at Scott." *New York Times* (August 15, 1994): D1, D2.

35 Nordheimer, J. "Downsized, but not out: A milltown's tale." *New York Times* (March 9, 1997): F1, F12–13.

36 Norris, F. "Chainsaw Al loses buzz on Wall Street." *International Herald-Tribune* (June 4, 1998): 13.

37 Brannigan, M. and J. R. Hagerty. "Sunbeam, its prospects looking ever worse, fires CEO Dunlap." *Wall Street Journal* (June 15, 1998): A1, A14.

38 Ibid.

39 Ibid. On May 16, 2001, the *New York Times* reported that Albert Dunlap and other associated with Sunbeam were accused by the Securities and Exchange Commission of accounting fraud.

40 Gilpin, K. N. "Ex Sunbeam executives to pay $15 Million to settle lawsuit." *New York Times* (January 15, 2002): C1, C2.

41 Burke, W.W. "The new agenda for organization development." *Organization Dynamics* (Summer, 1997): 1–14.

42 Keller, J. J. "AT&T will eliminate 40,000 jobs and take a charge of $4 billion." *Wall Street Journal* (January 3, 1996): A3, A6.; Keller, J. J. "AT&T's Robert Allen gets sharp criticism over layoffs, losses." *Wall Street Journal* (February 22, 1996): A1, A8.

43 Loomis, C. J. "AT&T has no clothes." *Fortune* (February 5, 1996): 78–80.

44 Andrews, E. L. "In AT&T's attic, $1 billion of flops and fumbles." *New York Times* (January 4, 1996): D1, D3.

45 Smith, L. "Burned-out bosses." *Fortune* (July 25, 1994): 44–52.

[46] Hagerty, J. R. and T. Parker-Pope. "A veteran Perelman fireman sets out to resuscitate Sunbeam." *Wall Street Journal* (June 6, 1998): B1, B3.

[47] Johnston, D. C. "At Levi Strauss a big cutback, with largess." *New York Times* (November 11, 1997): D1, D6.

[48] Ibid.

[49] Ligos, M. "The opposite of layoffs: Ties of loyalty." *New York Times* (January 20, 2002): BU1.

[50] Quintanilla, C. "A special news report about life on the job—and trends taking shape there." *Wall Street Journal* (May 27, 1997): 1.

[51] Noberg, D. "The human cost of restructuring." *Chicago Tribune* (March 2, 1988): 15.

[52] Brockner, J. and B. Wiesenfield. "Living on the edge of social and organizational psychology: The effects of job layoffs on those who remain." In K. Murnigham *Social Psychology in Organizations: Advances in Theory and Research.* Englewood Cliffs, NJ: Prentice-Hall, 1993.

[53] Greenberg, J. *The Quest for Justice on the Job.* Thousand Oaks, CA: Sage, 1996.

[54] Hymowitz, C. "Just how much should a boss reveal to others about a staffer's firing?" *Wall Street Journal* (March 19, 2002): B1.

[55] Greenberg, *The Quest for Justice on the Job.*

[56] Unequivocal evidence establishes that illogical or insincere communications do not have the same beneficial effects (*See* Greenberg, *The Quest for Justice on the Job*).

[57] Stanfield, R. E. "Job retraining: An answer to NAFTA?" *National Journal* 24 (1992): 2498–2499; Zippay, A. "The effects of advance notice on displaced manufacturing workers: A case study." *Labor Studies Journal* 18 (1993): 43.

[58] Bartel, A. "Productivity gains from the implementation of employee training programs." *Industrial Relations* 33 (1994): 411–425.

[59] Casio, "Guide to responsible restructuring."

[60] Lieber, R. B. "How safe is your job." *Fortune* (April 1, 1996): 72–80.

[61] Smith, V. C. "Retraining the troops." *Human Resource Executive* (July, 1995): 16–20.

[62] Casio, "Guide to responsible restructuring."

[63] Ibid.

[64] Brown, J. and D. Isaacs. "Building corporations as communities: The best of both worlds." In P. Senge, A. Kleiner, C. Roberts, R. Ross, and B. Smith (Eds.) *The Fifth Discipline Fieldbook.* New York: Doubleday, 1994: 69–83.

[65] Hammonds, K. H., W. Zeller, and R. Melcher. "Writing a new social contract." *Business Week* (March 11, 1996): 60–61.

[66] Ansberry, C. "In the new workplace job morph to suit rapid pace of change." *Wall Street Journal* (March 22, 2002): A1, A7.

[67] Appel, T. "A factory manager improvises to save jobs in a downturn." *Wall Street Journal* (December 27, 2001): A1, A4.

4

THE THIRD R—
RECOGNITION:
VOICE LESSONS

In 1996, 57 percent of the employees responding to a Delta Airlines internal survey said that the quality of customer service had declined during the previous two years. Forty-eight percent rated the effectiveness of Delta's leadership as "unfavorable," and 61 percent *disagreed* with the statement "management can be trusted."

This dismal display came from an employee group that once bought the company a new Boeing 767 they named "The Spirit of Delta." Analysts blamed the turnabout on Delta's strategy for cutting $2 billion from operating costs. "Leadership 7.5" was the strategy's name. The "7.5" referred to the airline's target for one of the industry's common financial indices: the cost of flying one seat one mile. Delta wanted to lower the cost to 7.5 cents from 9.6 cents; a target that Delta CEO Robert W. Allen acknowledged was a "stretch goal" during his April 2, 1994 news conference.[1]

During 1995, the year after Mr. Allen launched "Leadership 7.5," the plan was apparently working. With employees' help, vacation time was reduced, a cap had been placed on health benefits, there were improvements in cabin service, commissions to travel agents were cut, and customer service ratings remained high. By 1996–1997, however, about three years into the effort, outcomes took a nosedive. Adverse effects on employee morale and customer service emerged despite financial inducements, including the continued availability of robust severance packages.[2] Dollars were unable to squelch discontent. Observers contend that this was a time during which the company became increasingly less receptive to employees' inputs to "Leadership 7.5".[3] By muffling their voices, Delta turned once-supportive employees into aliens who felt little sense of common purpose with their employer.

The mid-1990s was not a financially easy time for airlines. During the same year that Delta conducted its internal survey, 1996, another airline, British Airways (BA), launched its "Business Efficiency" program, attempting to cut $1.69 billion in costs by the year 2000. The program, pretty much planned by senior management and then announced to the workforce, produced a predictable response. BA pilots threatened to walk out during the summer, peak travel time, and cabin crews actually waged a three-day strike reputed to have cost the airline $210 million. The events caused a *Wall Street Journal* reporter to observe, "…employee morale has sagged considerably, as passengers complain that smiles are fewer in a business where flashing teeth count."[4] Perhaps the final chapter of this part of the BA story occurred during the late winter of 2000, when the resignation of the firm's CEO, Robert Ayling, was evidently influenced by the staff's feelings of antagonism toward him.

On some occasions, failing to recognize employees by denying them opportunity to voice their views paradoxically prevents companies from learning ways to achieve the savings that they were seeking in the first place. According to Gary Hamel and C. K. Prahalad, this is precisely what happened to a U.S. company that was being financially battered by Far East competitors whose primary business weapon was lower labor costs.[5] A long, bitter strike that followed the U.S. company's attempt to wrest a 40 percent salary concession from its employees ended with an agreement that included a mere 10 percent concession. Since direct labor costs affected only 15 percent of the U.S. company's total value added, that 10 percent concession was worth a tiny 1.5 percent reduction in total costs to the company. "Ironically, further analysis showed that their competitors' most significant cost savings came not from lower hourly wages, but from better work methods *invented by employees* (italics added)."[6]

Giving employees voice obviously provides employers with opportunities for gleaning valuable ideas. Less obvious is the way the act of giving employees voice sends a message to them saying that they are trusted, valued, and competent. Silencing them smothers the ideas. It also says, "What *you* have to say is of no concern to *us*." In employees' minds, that exclusionary message propels the organization icon across the *we/they* boundary, deep into *they* territory.

The value of giving workers voice has been steadily demonstrated in behavioral science research for at least two-thirds of a century. In the mid-1970s, the mid-1980s, and the mid-1990s[7], reviews of this research all reached the same conclusion: *Employees are more apt to accept rules arising from decisions if they have had genuine opportunities to affect the decision-making. In comparison to their silenced counterparts, these employees have better productivity, more favorable work relationships, and a greater sense of personal well being.*

Be careful not to misinterpret the implications of these conclusions. Giving employees a genuine opportunity to influence does not require bosses to either surrender control over outcomes or invite inputs on any and all matters. Employees are folks like you and I. Most of us realize that no one is entitled to sway all decisions.

We might be disappointed not to get our own way, but empirical evidence and experience make it clear that the benefits of voice do occur when employees are given the opportunity to speak and have reason to believe that bosses are truly considering their views. Employees certainly welcome decision outcomes that favor them, but despite anyone's views to the contrary, a favorable outcome is not a prerequisite to achieving the gains that voice has to offer. When there are genuine opportunities for employees to exercise voice, the benefits frequently occur even when bosses' final decisions run counter to employee self-interest.[8]

Donald E. Peterson, Ford Motor Company's former CEO, showed his understanding of these issues when he wrote about "participative management," one of the many different labels that has been used to describe times when employees have opportunities to voice their views. He defined participative management as "simply a style of operating in which you give your peers and subordinates an opportunity to say what they think, and you include their ideas in the overall decision-making process."[9]

Organizations that follow CEO Donald Peterson's prescription, to bring to decision making the views that were voiced by peers and subordinates, communicate their regard for employees. *We* is created. And with its creation comes the psychological golden rule of organizations: *Harming you becomes difficult for me because the two of us are part of* we. Once this rule is operating, it becomes the basis for better *productivity*, more favorable *work relationships*, and even a greater sense of personal *well being.*

Voice and Productivity

After Doreen Dickey accepted a job with Foldcraft Corporation, a company located in Kenyon, Minnesota that makes restaurant furniture, "she expected that scraping and sanding excess sealant for seats would bore and alienate her." Fortunately, because of Foldcraft's approach to management, that expectation was never fulfilled. The company first took steps to educate Ms. Dickey about the industry and then it sought her input about modifying work processes related to her responsibilities. Instead of her being bored and alienated, Doreen Dickey's productivity rose. Reflecting back she said that her "...head was spinning with ideas on how to make my job better."[10]

When Foldcraft Corporation's management invited Ms. Dickey to voice her views, they sent her a message of inclusion. Her response, and no doubt that from many other Foldcraft employees as well, was inclusion of the organization on the *we* side of the *we/they* boundary. Once *we* is established and the golden rule of organizations is operating, employees are partners. Their standard of performance becomes "What outcomes are favorable to *us*?" When bosses exile employees to *they*, the golden rule is cancelled and employees' standard of performance becomes "What outcomes are favorable to *me*?"

Opportunities for employees to voice their views saved Hannaford Brothers, a retail food company, $500,000 in compensation costs resulting from injuries. At Miller Brewing, a similar opportunity yielded a 30 percent reduction in labor costs and associated increases in productivity. And, at Texas Instruments, change attributed to management's recognition of employees' voices caused customer returns to drop to .03 percent from 3 percent.[11]

Eaton Corporation's 35,000 employees manufacture gear parts, axles, circuit breakers, and valves for engines at 80 sites across the United States and Canada. The firm's stress on employee voice evidently paid off. In 1992, ideas contributed by one of Eaton's Lincoln, Nebraska plant workers were instrumental in producing a $1.4 million savings.[12]

High functioning work teams are a quintessential setting in which employees have opportunity to voice their views. Evidence gathered over many years, in different industries, constantly attests to the success of teams as a means of raising work productivity. Proctor and Gamble's team-based plants get between 30 percent and 40 percent higher productivity than their more traditional counterparts; a self-directed team at Tektronix Inc. reduced 14 days of work on a particular work process to

3 days; teams at Shenandoah Life, working with 10 percent fewer employees than comparable work units, turn out 50 percent more work; and a 13 percent improvement in service at Federal Express is attributable to the company's use of teams.[13]

Dana Corporation is an automobile parts manufacturer with headquarters in Toledo, Ohio and plants in Mexico, Kentucky, Missouri, and Pennsylvania. In 1996, the company's 45,000 employees produced 666,120 suggestions, an average of 1.2 suggestions per employee per month. They ranged from ideas concerning manufacturing processes (place a small weld on steel sheets so that they can be piled and automatically loaded into a forming press—saving a quarter of a million dollars) to improvements in the parking situation (stagger work schedules to make it unnecessary to spend $110,000 on expanding parking lot space).[14] Why does Dana Corporation's suggestion system succeed when so many others end up as no more than empty, unused boxes mounted on company walls? The answer is "voice." Dana takes suggestions seriously, giving employees' responsibility for assessing and implementing them.[15]

Evidently, the production of creative ideas is at least as much a consequence of inclusion as it is of employees' individual abilities. In fact, R&D scientists, who were questioned about what produces innovative ideas, responded straightforwardly that their productivity was enhanced most in settings where they had a sense of freedom rather than constraint.[16] Organizations that silence employees' voices decrease the likelihood of gleaning innovative ideas from them, even if they hire them for their intelligence and enroll them in training programs that promise to improve each participant's capacity for *left-brain, outside of the box, lateral thinking.*

Organization attempts to increase productivity by redesigning either individual jobs or the job composition of whole work units also fall short of their potential if they fail to properly recognize the role of voice. Two decades ago, behavioral scientists investigating the effects of what continues to be a popular management strategy, *job enrichment*, showed that engineering jobs had less benefit if employees were excluded from, rather than enrolled in, the redesign process. When enrollment gave employees an opportunity to voice their views, it heightened their feelings about work's meaningfulness as well as their knowledge of work outcomes and sense of responsibility for them.[17] These positive effects of enrollment led directly to increases in workers' commitment and loyalty.

Sadly, these discoveries were forgotten a decade later when *business process re-engineering* swept through the work world. (*Business process re-engineering* is an organization redesign tool that replaces work units that are organized and staffed along lines of functional responsibility, such as engineering, marketing, finance, with units that are organized around key work processes, such as customer service, and staffed with personnel from all relevant functions.) In many companies, this organization redesign tool became little more than a "business correct" excuse for firing employees after senior management installed a leaner organization that was designed and dictated by them.

A steady stream of failures jolted both users and creators of re-engineering to remind the business community that simply dropping payroll costs by unilaterally cutting jobs does not yield the benefits promised by this tool. Replacing those benefits are employee resistance, little buy-in, and lots of bail out. Eventually, re-engineering experts like Michael Hammer and James Champy explicitly called for more attention to what they called the "people" issues, meaning that if you are going to re-engineer, involve employees early, often, and honestly; don't re-engineer *them*.[18]

The use of rewards in order to overcome the negative reactions of silenced employees frequently meets the same unhappy fate as efforts to re-engineer jobs around *them*. Certainly, one of the most remarkable findings to emerge from thousands of investigations of organizational phenomena is that identical levels of rewards are judged in entirely opposite ways depending on whether employees receiving those rewards had opportunities to influence the decisions that produced them. Specifically, employees with opportunities for voice make favorable judgments of the very same rewards than those denied the opportunities judge unfavorably.[19]

But more than employee judgement is affected when employees are given or denied opportunities for voice. A comparison of work groups that influenced the development of their own pay plans with work groups that had *the very same pay plans imposed on them* showed that work attendance increased for those with voice. For employees lacking voice, attendance actually grew worse. This difference, first observed after 16 weeks, still existed after one year. [20]

Other evidence shows that problems associated with the use of gain-sharing plans, such as free riding by some employees, are reduced when workers participate in designing the plan's rules. In fact, the power of giving workers voice is so great that even the passive, limited voice offered by companies' cafeteria plans has small but clearly positive effects on employee satisfaction and commitment.[21]

Success in tying rewards to productivity through performance appraisals is also affected by the degree to which the appraisal process gives employees genuine opportunities to voice their views. Concern about performance appraisal has traditionally focused on its measurement accuracy. This concern probably grew because performance appraisals primarily have been designed to answer three questions: Is our organization getting what it needs from workers? Are differences in contribution being assessed and tied to rewards? Does the appraisal's paper trail provide us with legal protection?[22]

Without diminishing the importance of improving this tool's precision, the fact is that performance appraisals have more positive effects on employees when bosses solicit and use employees' input prior to making appraisal-related decisions, engage employees in discussion during appraisal meetings, and recognize their freedom to question the evaluation.[23] Bosses, who discourage discussion by using the appraisal process as a time to tell subordinates what they did well or poorly and how to fix *their* errors, set themselves up as an elite. In their hands, performance appraisals become messages of exclusion sent by a lofty *us* to a lowly *them*.

Voice and Work Relationships

Bosses know that it is important to earn their employees' trust. But they do not always know how to go about getting it. The fact is, that if bosses want to raise the level of subordinates' trust in them, they probably need to pay as much, and perhaps more, attention to how they are managing employee voice than as to how they are managing tasks. Investigations repeatedly reveal that workers' trust in their bosses is more closely tied to their judgments about whether bosses consider their views, take their needs into account during decision making, and discuss decisions with them, than it is to their bosses' efforts to solve current problems or prevent future ones.[24] Because boss-subordinate relationships lacking in trust have been a documented cause of business failure, paying more attention to how voice is being managed could offer bosses practical dividends. Evidence from government agencies and business firms around the world indicates that more trusting boss-subordinate relationships are associated with higher levels of performance.[25]

Two nearly opposite consequences of employees' lack of trust in bosses contribute to erosion of their performance. One occurs when coworkers band together in order to combat a common enemy: their untrustworthy boss. The resulting work disruption is produced by their wasted energy, efforts at undermining someone that they mistrust, and occasional outright sabotage. The second outcome occurs when employees, who want to avoid their untrustworthy boss' displeasure, seek to become the boss' favorite by combating one another. To the victor go the spoils. Do better than one's peers and dangers decline; do worse than they do and the dangers will increase. Once these competitive reward contingencies have been established, *we* shrinks as former members of *us* become one another's targets. It is a work circumstance in which basically good people become capable of doing very bad things.

Jane's success is Jim's failure. Their boss has made them adversaries. Fearing one another's accomplishments, each seeks safety by accumulating triumphs and erecting a prudent defense (commonly referred to in organizations as PYA, or "protect your ass"). But instead of making her feel safe, Jane's victories and her PYA defenses simply (and realistically) increase her worries about Jim's retaliation. Sadly, with each downward spiral the circle of *we* grows smaller until it is no larger than *"I,"* ending any semblance of collaborative working relationships.

Voice and Employee Well Being

The *"I"* remaining in the employ of a boss who has stifled voice is likely to have diminished well being. More than a quarter of a century ago, in 1973, a special task force delivered a report to the Secretary of Health, Education, and Welfare called *Work in America*. This report summarized hundreds of investigations proving that "work plays a crucial and unparalleled role in the formation of self-esteem, identity, and a sense of order."[26] Magnifying the importance of this conclusion is evidence linking workers' self-esteem to a long list of health-related symptoms.

In comparison to their high self-esteem counterparts, employees with low self-esteem show more anxiety, depression, and neurotic behavior. When under stress, they work less well, exhibit poorer social skills, and are less friendly. Employees with lower self-esteem are also more compliant and less aspiring. Their expectations of success are lower than those of coworkers with high self-esteem, as are their initiative and assertiveness.[27]

This does not mean that every worker's self-esteem is equally vulnerable to experiences at work. There is no reason to doubt that some folks show up at an organization's door with rather durable high or low levels of self-esteem. But there is also no reason to doubt that for a large part of the workforce, being uplifted or downtrodden all day long, each and every workday, slowly elevates or erodes pre-existing levels of self-esteem. The means for raising or lowering workers' self-esteem are no mystery. Employees' self-esteem grows or declines because of social interaction. Pay, the evidence tells us, has nothing to do with it.[28] One authority on the subject of self-esteem at work, Columbia University's Business School Professor Joel Brockner, summed it up by saying that the "more individual work roles require them to act in a 'high self-esteem manner' … the greater will be their self-esteem."[29] Giving employees voice sends a message affirming their capability. It tells them that they are trusted and valued, and it affords them many opportunities to act in a high self-esteem manner. Stifling voice sends the opposite message, denying them those opportunities.

Of course, employees' self-esteem is also affected by interaction with coworkers. But every indicator points to bosses' behavior as, by far, the predominant influence. If bosses' behavior is respectful, affirming subordinates' dignity, then subordinates' self-esteem is enhanced; if it is not, then self-esteem is more likely to be harmed.

In one study, hundreds of working men and women rated their bosses' relationships with them, including the degree to which the bosses cared, supported, and appreciated subordinates. Bosses who were caring, supportive, and appreciative had subordinates with higher self-esteem. (Just for the record, the correlation between the two was .29.) In comparison, the relationship between boss behavior and both depression and anxiety was negative. (The correlations between them were −.57 and −.47, respectively.)[30] Less caring, supportive, or appreciative boss behavior was associated with greater subordinate depression and anxiety.

Even more dramatic is evidence indicating that unsupportive boss behavior might be a contributor to the occurrence of heart disease.[31] Very simply, this means that levels of psychological and physical well being are likely to be greater for workers whose bosses offer them genuine invitations to exercise voice.

Voice Recognition

Methods of denying employees genuine opportunities to exercise voice come in many disguises. Brian Graves, a petrochemical company executive, sounded exasperated when he spoke about his boss' deceit.

> *Saying, "My door is always open" doesn't mean a*
> *damn thing if 90 percent of the time what you get is*
> *mushroom management. (You know—keeping you in the*
> *dark under a cover of fertilizer.) Let's face it; you hear*
> *that all the time. First of all, it's not always an honest*
> *invitation. For some, the last thing in the world that they*
> *want is for you to come marching through the door to*
> *talk with them about what's going on. Second, they*
> *make sure that can't happen by not giving you the full*
> *picture. I mean—it's a control thing—if you don't know*
> *what's happening or where the firm is heading, there's*
> *not much that you can say. Right?*

Brian is right. Permission to speak is fraudulent if employees lack information, freedom to act, or an understanding of the organization's intended direction.

Voice and Information

Withholding information—keeping employees in the dark—is one obvious way to undermine their opportunity to exercise voice. A less obvious scheme uses a steady stream of information to inundate employees with detailed marching orders. By constantly telling them what to do and when to do it, bosses are also saying "Follow the bouncing ball. Expressions of voice are not invited."

7-Eleven point-of-sale computer systems are capable of monitoring shopkeepers' work activities as well as customers' buying habits. They record the time that shopkeepers spend using the system's capacities to scrutinize sales' data, customer demography, and weather forecasts for their inventory implications (e.g., stock umbrellas for rainy days and bottles of water for an upcoming hot spell). The system beeps warnings in order to alert shopkeepers to order goods, and it triggers headquarters personnel to issue warnings to 7-Eleven shop workers who disregard the system's signals.

One shopkeeper who quit his job with 7-Eleven in order to buy a franchise and become his own boss complained about his work experience with the company. *Sometimes I don't know who's really running the store.... It's like being under 24-hour surveillance; it's like being enslaved.* The author of this grievance is Michiharo Endo. The franchise that he owns, and the 7-Eleven that he quit, are both located in Japan.[32]

Instead of driving work, 7-Eleven's use of information appears to have driven some employees out of the organization. Mark Challenger, CEO of U.S. Office Equipment Inc., a photocopier distributor based in Illinois, has a different view about how information should be used. U.S. Office Equipment salespeople are free to request internal data when they need it, without restriction. *"When all the information is available,* explained Mr. Challenger, *not just what the company wants them to have— they make much more intelligent decisions."*[33]

There is always some organizational information that is unsuitable for unrestricted public disclosure. But there is always peril when bosses decide where to draw a line between what information can be shared and what information should be kept secret.[34] Bosses' decisions to withhold information do not simply handicap employees' problem solving. Regardless of anyone's intentions, those being kept in the dark easily interpret this denial of information as a message declaring that *they* are not anointed members of the organization's elite.

This is precisely what seems to have happened several years ago when AT&T was searching for someone to succeed President Alex J. Mandl and, eventually, Chairman Robert Allen. The choice, John R. Walter, was kept a secret. Evidently, the exclusion was upsetting to both senior executives and lower-level managers. One of them observed that the secrecy communicated "We don't care what you think, you're dispensable, especially if you're middle level."[35]

Voice and the Freedom to Act

When Canon decided to outpace Xerox in the personal copier business, it challenged its engineers with the task of creating a home copier that sold for $1,000 or less. Then it freed them to achieve that goal. They came through for their employer by inventing a disposable cartridge that replaced the more expensive device used in competitors' products.

Monarch Marking Systems, a company that produces bar-coding and other price-marking materials, introduced similar autonomy for its employees, but with a twist. For its 500 workers, participation in autonomous problem-solving teams was mandatory.

Monarch measures its work activity using 162 metrics. Teams were given responsibility for one of these metrics each and were charged with the task of developing and implementing action plans that would lead to their metric's improvement. Consideration of "soft" matters for which there were no objective measures (e.g., "How can we improve collaboration?") were excluded from the agenda. Consequently, there was no need for subjective judgment in evaluating Monarch's teams' successes. One group reduced "the number of job categories to 32 from 120 through cross-training." A second team cut the setup time involved in a label-making operation by 25 percent. Another eliminated 7,600 staff hours by changing the existing procedures for reporting production. And a fourth team "reduced square footage of their assembly area 70 percent, cut work-in-progress inventory by $127,000, and slashed past due shipments 90 percent...."[36]

The reason why Monarch's approach works is, in the words of one employee, "We're not just pieces of equipment anymore.... My input means something."

In 1996, Les Alberthal, CEO of Electronic Data Systems (EDS), who was once described in *Fortune* magazine as a "tough guy who wants to give you a hug"[37] said, "We have historically been dominated by two brands—Perot and GM. This is the first time we have had to develop our own identity 100 percent tied to the company." (EDS' history began in 1962 when Ross Perot founded it. He sold it to GM in 1988, and GM sold it to shareholders in June 1996.) Mr. Alberthal wanted to move the company from what he and many others saw as a rigid, military command and control culture to one with greater employee autonomy, permitting more sensitivity and responsiveness to customers.

In addition to training sessions designed to stimulate the development of this more open culture, EDS restructured its decision-making processes. Gary Fernandez, the company's vice chairman, described the restructuring by explaining, "We've moved from a cult of personality to a culture where the emphasis is on teams arriving at collective decisions." In the eyes of employees like Sally Mattei, a supervisor with responsibility for 750 employees, this move toward autonomy was working. She said, "As a manager, I used to pride myself that I was taking more personal responsibility than anybody. That made me like a dictator." When things at work went wrong, Ms. Mattei's response was, "You did wrong; we need to learn from this. Everybody see this mistake that was made. Now go fix it."[38]

Reflecting back on how she and EDS once were, she concluded, "All that did was alienate people from me. Yes, the problem got fixed. But my team did it begrudgingly." As a result, they performed less well than they could have. With the move toward greater autonomy, Sally Mattei explains, she gets better results by coordinating team efforts at analysis of problems and generation of solutions.

As EDS had hoped, its move toward more employee autonomy has also benefited business operations in relation to customers. Dennis Roy, a manager in Iowa, explains that contract negotiations with customers were times during which employees would try to one-up each other. The resulting sessions in Mr. Roy's view caused relationships with customers to deteriorate. With the changes at EDS, however, "we've eliminated hidden agendas on both sides. Meetings start by asking, 'What do you want to accomplish out of this deal?'.... In Dennis Roy's judgment "negotiations are faster, more likely to be win-win, and result in additional business opportunity." Marsha Clark, head of EDS training, observes, "This is not about harmony, but about having voice and feeling that your contributions are valued."[39]

As a vice president at Staples, Inc., the office supply retailer, Jane Biering worked in the catalogue division where clerks fill customer orders using a network of warehouses and distribution hubs. Outside her office hung a sign that announced an elegantly simple prescription for success. It read, *"Let the people who are closest to the work improve the way things work."*[40]

Following that rule of voice, Ms. Biering had supervisors of operators move from secluded offices to cubicles placed among the folks they supervised, bosses met weekly with their teams, and customer service personnel, whose job required them to regularly resolve problems with hub managers, moved to hub locations. By having employees who need to work together assembled in common physical settings, Biering provided them greater opportunity to understand one another's work pressures and priorities, promoting a mentality of *us*, instead of one featuring *you* versus *me*.

The outcomes experienced by Canon, Monarch Marking Systems, EDS, and Staples are not unique. Almost invariably, evidence published in scientific journals reports that employees who are given a chance to speak about assigned goals believe that they are being treated more fairly and are more likely to accept those goals and work well than employees who are denied opportunities to speak. Remarkably, the power of voice to produce these positive outcomes persists even when the goals that are eventually assigned are not the ones that were initially preferred by employees.[41] Indeed, there is evidence that even when final decisions fall short of employees' preferences, they are more willing to forgo acting on self-interest if they participated in group discussions about the decisions than if they were excluded from those discussions.[42]

Voice and Direction

Aside from occupying the CEO's office in their respective organizations, what did Andy Grove (Intel), Roger Enrico (Pepsico), Jack Welch (General Electric), and Admiral Ray Smith (United States Special Operations Command) have in common? One answer, according to Eli Cohen and Noel Tichy, is that they all had an active involvement in teaching other members of their organizations what is required in order to lead those institutions toward success. Jack Welch, for example, acknowledges, "I've been to Crotonville [GE's training facility in Westchester County, NY] every two weeks for 15 years to interact with new (employees), middle managers, and senior managers. Haven't missed a session."[43]

Too many bosses in other organizations learn about what these successful CEOs have done and then decide that they too will send a message to their employees, telling them what organization success requires. Missing a very important point, these copycat bosses communicate their ideas through memos, newsletters, and nowadays, even through e-mail. What they have failed to understand is that Andy Grove and the others have impact not just because of what they say as teachers, which might be wise, but also because of how they go about delivering their messages. Instead of making elite, pontifical pronouncements from the isolation of a boss' office, they go into the pit. Their way of working is face to face. They use a hands-on approach to send an inclusive message that says, *You're worth it!* Standing in the pit, these bosses risk, and often even invite role reversal. It causes them to become listeners rather than speakers, learners who are also teachers. It makes them more human, vulnerable, and a part of their employees' *we*.

David Sullivan, chief operating officer of Promus Hotel Corporation, a Memphis, Tennessee company that manages Embassy Suites, Hampton Inns, and Homewood Suites, profited by putting himself in the position of a teacher who is also a learner. He did it by giving employees a telephone number that they could call in order to chat with him. The conversations led to positive, practical changes, like revising the pay scale for employees taking reservations, as well as to improvements in employees' feelings about the Promus Hotel Corporation. Mr. Sullivan's comment was "We'll do it again. It makes everybody feel good, including me."[44]

The technique of "360-degree feedback" also can erect bonds of *we* between bosses and employees by creating a time when bosses are "in the pit." The tool's label, *360-degree*, captures the idea that, in theory, feedback to each and every organization member about his or her work activity should come from a *full circle* of coworkers, including bosses, subordinates, peers, and self. When it operates perfectly, employees, from the hierarchy's top to its bottom, receive information about their work from colleagues in all the surrounding perspectives. They are then able to compare the others' inputs to their own views, identify areas for improvement, and take appropriate action. When the technique is carried out in this fashion, bosses and subordinates alike become learners and teachers. Unfortunately, in practice, the ideal is rarely realized. According to a recent report, full 360-degree feedback occurs in a mere 12 percent of U.S. organizations.[45]

Many claim that the feedback's purpose is to produce an "accurate self-perception" and a "valid picture of strengths and weaknesses." The claim is exaggerated. When differences in feedback exist, the minority might be correct and the majority wrong, or the reverse. And when the circle of viewpoints coalesces, it is still no guarantee of either their accuracy or their validity. Reporters might simply be sharing a popular myth. But these liabilities of 360-degree feedback should not cause great consternation. While the tool's power might be augmented by accuracy, it is not totally dependent on it.

Feedback—90-degree, 180-degree, or 360-degree—is about questions, not answers. It is about developing a healthy sense of respect for employees whom the process endorses as important, respected repositories of information about work performance. Psychologically, this endorsement narrows the gap among levels of organization hierarchy. At the very least, it does this by encouraging bosses to become learners who attend to what others say about them. If occupants of all levels of the hierarchy receive 360-degree feedback, then the process itself proclaims that every employee must constantly assess and improve. No one, no matter what his or her position might be, is ever entirely finished with those tasks. Their common imperfection, and the way in which the feedback process fosters reliance on others for improvement, is a great equalizer, encouraging bonds of *we*.

When feedback is constrained, however, with powerful members of organizations exempting themselves from the process, the results are very different. It establishes bosses as an elite *us* who assert that *we need no further learning or improvement*, and everyone else as a lesser *them*, whose improvements will be prescribed by the elite, boss, *us*.

Not Voice Alone

Organizations that afford employees voice, information, autonomy, and direction are not free of problems. On one occasion, factory workers who were given more freedom to act on their own required coworkers who committed offenses to appear before the entire workforce in order to "tell their side of the story." After listening, the workforce voted in order to arrive at a decision about whether the offenders would remain on the job. It happened twice, was judged ineffective, and ended. The plant, which won a quality award, had a manager whose comment on the episode was, "You run self-direction by trial and error.... and we decided that didn't work"[46]

Levi, the apparel maker, also had experiences with increased worker autonomy that did not work. In 1998, some of Levi's factory workers were assigned to teams that were given more authority over their own actions. In order to support the change, the company's reward structure shifted to one that paid for team performance from one that paid for individual piecework. The change produced some benefit. For example, teams improved turnaround by reducing the interval between the time when orders were received and the time that shipments were made. But along with these gains came problems. Incivility among peers grew. Team members threatened one another when they suspected poor performance, or if they judged others' restroom visits to be overly frequent. Teasing, resentment, and stress climbed to a point where work declined. "Former managers and Levi consultants say that executives bungled the transition by giving insufficient guidance to supervisors on how to implement the system."[47] Without disagreeing, Levi's chairman and CEO, Mr. Robert Haas, wisely admitted, "Ours is a culture of experimentation and innovation and novelty, and we're not always successful."[48] Welcome to the human race.

No matter how work is arranged, problems will arise. Better solutions to problems simply reduce their frequency and boost an organization's speed of recovery. Increased voice for employees expands the marketplace of useful ideas while reducing any one group's power to compel all the rest to waste time following a futile course of action just because more powerful people have made public commitments to it.

But, this does not mean that organizations function best as leaderless anarchies. Employees, who are given voice, even if it is accompanied by information and autonomy, will remain ineffective if organization leadership provides no direction. Canon did not say to its engineers, "When work permits, it might be useful to gather in order to chat about ways of improving some things around here." Canon said to them, "We want to surpass competitors. Design a personal copier that will sell for under $1,000." *The problem in organizations is not the establishment of rules; it is an establishment that rules.*

Charisma and Voice

Some leaders are lucky. A combination of their communication skills, intuition, and institutional circumstance allows them to formulate messages that capture other employees' core concerns, giving these other employees vicarious expression of voice. These lucky few have been called "transformational leaders."[49] In one fell swoop their messages express direction and erect ties that bind.

"*Transactional* leaders" have an entirely different impact on listeners. Their messages appeal to immediate, instrumental needs. In their relationships with subordinates, concerns about utility and self-interest replace the transformational leaders' arousal of inspiration and initiative. Transactional leaders implicitly bargain, *Give me what I need and you will get what you need in return.* Paychecks and punishment might get performance, occasionally even excellent performance, but they are not a basis for the deep, enduring feelings of commitment and loyalty produced by transformational leaders.

As if in response to evidence about the powerful effects of transformational leaders, organizations have set about writing what they hope will be engaging "mission" statements. Knight-Ridder Inc., the publishing giant, identifies itself as the "preeminent deliverer of information services," and Xerox calls itself "the document company."[50] Organization mottos, metaphors, and credos such as these are potentially useful, because they identify the organization's preferred direction, but they lack the binding effect of a transformational statement. None come close to have the engaging power of Martin Luther King's ringing refrain, "I have a dream."

Problems created by this lack of impact are compounded when mission statements are composed in remote organization confines with inputs from just a few select senior managers. That sadly familiar process turns the workforce into a passive, voiceless observer of an elite's decisions. If the mission statement that they decide on somehow strikes the right chord, then workers might get turned on, accept the goals, and get on with supporting work effort. But if the chord that is struck is anything less than harmonious with employees' desires, then their listening will decline as the gulf between *them and us* grows.

Only a few people have charisma. Even if organizations could accurately pinpoint these few by using recruitment and selection tools that do *not* currently exist, there still would not be enough charismatic leaders to go around. The personal gifts and organizational circumstances that are necessary ingredients for creating this special leadership experience are not commonplace. Most of us are more ordinary people who dwell amidst more ordinary circumstance.

But no one needs to despair. Seventy-five years of scientific inquiry and approximately two centuries of modern management experience contain hundreds of practical examples of what can be done by bosses who sincerely want to build bonds of *we* between employees and their employing institution by attending to the three **R**s of organization life (**R**ewards, **R**espect, and **R**ecognition). How that can happen, and the rewarding outcomes that occur when it does, are the next chapter's focus, *"What money can't buy, and how to buy it."*

[1] Bryant, A. "What price efficiency?" *New York Times* (July 25, 1997): D1, D6.

[2] Ibid.

[3] Ibid.

[4] Goldsmith, C. "British Air profits fall as criticism mounts." *Wall Street Journal* (November 24, 1997): A19.

[5] Hamel, G. and C. K. Prahalad. "Strategic intent." *Harvard Business Review* (May–June, 1989): 63–76.

[6] Ibid., 68.

[7] Katzell, R. A. and D. Yanklovitich. "Work productivity and job satisfaction: An evaluation of policy related research." New York: Psychological Corporation, 1975; Lawler, E. E. "Choosing an involvement strategy." *Academy of Management* II. 1988:3, 197–204.; Guzzo, R. A. "Productivity research: Reviewing psychological and economic perspectives." In J. P. Campbell, R. J. Campbell, and Associates (Eds.) *Productivity in Organizations: New Perspectives from Industry and Organizational Psychology* (San Francisco, CA: Jossey-Bass, 1988): 63–81; Casio, W. F. "Wither industrial and organizational psychology in a changing world of work?" *American Psychologist* 50 (November, 1995): 928–939.

[8] Tyler, T. R. "The psychology of procedural justice: A test of the group-value model." *Journal of Personality and Social Psychology* 57 (1989): 830–838.; Tyler, T. R. "Psychological models of the justice motive: Antecedents of distributive and procedural justice." *Journal of Personality and Social Psychology* 67 (1994): 850–863.

[9] Peterson, D. E. and J. Hillkirk. *A Better Idea.* Boston: Houghton Mifflin Co., 1991.

[10] Zachary, G. P. "The new search for meaning is 'meaningless' work." *Wall Street Journal* (January 9, 1997): B1, B2.

[11] Byham, W. C. "Congress should strengthen the corporate team." *Wall Street Journal* (February 5, 1996): A14.

[12] Casio, "Wither industrial and organizational psychology in a changing world of work?"

[13] Hackman, J. R. "Why teams don't work." In R. S. Tindal, J. S. Edwards, and E. J. Posavac (Eds.) *Applications of Theory and Research on Groups to Social Issues* (New York: Plenum, 1997); Hackman, J. R. *Leading Teams*. Harvard Business School Press, 2002.

[14] Teitelbaum, R. "How to harness gray matter." *Fortune* (June 9, 1997): 168.

[15] Similar success are reported in Flaherty, J. "Suggestions rise from floors of U.S. factories." *New York Times* (April 18, 2001): P1.

[16] Michela, J. L. "Social psychology and organizations." In G. R. Semin and K. Fiedler (Eds.) *Applied Social Psychology* (London: Sage, 1996).

[17] Hackman J. R. and G. R. Oldham. *Work Redesign* (Reading, MA: Addison-Wesley, 1980).

[18] White, J. B. "Re-engineering gurus take steps to remodel their stalling vehicles." *Wall Street Journal* (November 26, 1996): A1, A3.

[19] For a summary, see Greenberg, J. *The Quest for Justice on the Job*. Thousand Oaks, CA: Sage, 1996.

[20] Lawler, E. E. and J. R. Hackman. "The impact of employee participation in the development of pay incentive plans: A field experiment." *Journal of Applied Psychology* 53 (1969): 467–471.

[21] Folger, R. and J. Greenberg. "Procedural justice: An interpretive analysis of personnel system." In G. R. Ferris and K. M. Rowland (Eds.) *Research in Personnel and Human Resource Management* III (Greenwich, CT: JAI, 1985): 141–183.

[22] Landy, F. J. and J. L. Farr. *The Measurement of Work Performance* (New York: Academic Press, 1983); Ghorpade, J. and M. M. Chen. "Creating quality-driven performance appraisal systems." *Academy of Management Executive* 9 (1995): 32–39.; Mohrman, A. M., S. M. Resnick-West, and E. E. Lawler. *Designing Performance Appraisal Systems: Aligning Appraisals and Organizational Realities* (San Francisco: Jossey-Bass Publishers, 1989); Murphy, K. R. and J. N. Cleveland. *Performance Appraisal: An Organizational Perspective* (Boston: Allyn & Bacon, 1991).

[23] Greenberg, *The Quest for Justice on the Job*.

[24] Tyler, T. R. and E. A. Lind. "A relational model of authority in groups." In *Advances in Experimental Social Psychology*, ed. M. Zanna (New York: Academic Press, 1992), 25: 115–191.

[25] LaPorta, R., F. Lopez-de-Salanes, A. Shleifer, and R. Vishny. Faculty research working paper series, John F. Kennedy School of Government, Harvard University (January, 1997): R97-03; Putnam, R. *Making Democracy Work: Civic Traditions in Modern Italy* (Princeton, NJ: Princeton University Press, 1993).

[26] "Work in America Report of special task force to the Secretary of health, education, and welfare." (Cambridge, Mass: MIT Press, 1973): 4.

27 Tharenou, P. "Employee self-esteem: A review of the literature." *Journal of Vocational Behavior* 15 (1979): 316–346.

28 Kohn, M. L. and C. Schooler. "Job conditions and personality: A longitudinal assessment of their reciprocal effects." *American Journal of Sociology* 87 (1982): 1257–1286.

29 Brockner, J. *Self-Esteem at Work* (Lexington, MA: Lexington Books, 1988).

30 Repetti, R. L. "Individual and common components of the social environment at work and psychological well-being." *Journal of Personality and Social Psychology* 52 (1987): 710–720.

31 Michela, J., D. H. Flint, and A. M. Lynch. "Disrespectful supervisory behavior as a social-environmental stressor at work." Paper presented at APA/NIOST Work Stress Conference (November, 1992).

32 Shirouze, N. and J. Bigness. "7-Eleven operators resist system to monitor managers." *Wall Street Journal* (June 16, 1997): B1, B3.

33 Petzinger, T. Jr. "Are you still clinging to those chestnuts of business? Read on." *Wall Street Journal* (May 9, 1997): B1.

34 Hymowitz, C. "Managers must respond to employee concerns about honest business." *Wall Street Journal* (February 19, 2002): B1.

35 Thomas, P. "Business Bulletin." *Wall Street Journal* (October 29, 1996): A1.

36 Petzinger, T. Jr. "Forget empowerment, this job requires constant brain power." *Wall Street Journal* (October 17, 1997): B1.

37 Kirkpatrick, D. "This tough guy wants to give you a hug." *Fortune* (October 14, 1996): 170–178.

38 Ibid.

39 Ibid.

40 Petzinger, T. Jr. "Jane Biering tells managers at Staples to lead by listening." *Wall Street Journal* (March 15, 1996): B1.

41 Tyler and Lind, "A relational model of authority in groups."

42 Kerr, N. L., J. Garst, D. A. Lewandowski, and S. A. Harris. "That still, small voice: Commitment to cooperate as an internalized versus a social norm." *Personality and Social Psychology Bulletin* 23 (1997): 1300–1311.

43 Cohen, E. and N. Tichy. "How leaders develop leaders." *Training and Development* (May 1997).

44 *Wall Street Journal* (October 24, 1996): A1.

45 Waldman, D. A., L. E. Atwater, and D. Antonioni. "Has 360 degree feedback gone amok?" *Academy of Management Executive* 12 (1998): 86–94.

46 Appel, T. "Not all workers find the idea of empowerment neat as it sounds." *Wall Street Journal* (September 8, 1997): A1, A10.

47 King, R. T. Jr. "Levi's factory workers are assigned to teams, and morale takes a hit." *Wall Street Journal* (May 20, 1998): A1, A6.

[48] Ibid.

[49] Burns, J. M. *Leadership* (New York: Harper & Row, 1978); Zaleznik, A. "Managers and leaders: Are they different?" *Harvard Business Review* 55 (1977): 67–78.

[50] Wishart, N. A., J. J. Elam, and D. Robey. "Redrawing the portrait of a learning organization: Inside Knight-Rider, Inc." *Academy of Management Executive* 10 (1996): 1, 7–20.

5

WHAT MONEY CAN'T BUY, AND HOW TO BUY IT: CHANGING BOSSES' MESSAGES

"Runs-on-schedule" is a measure of success commonly used by steel manufacturers. Investigations using this index have found that a mill's success is heavily affected by how well it is managing the three Rs of organization life: Rewards, Respect, and Recognition. Specifically, the management package that is characteristic of plants with near-perfect records of successful "runs-on-schedule" contains gain sharing, a plentiful array of opportunities for training, employment security, and the use of teams to solve work problems. Ninety-eight percent of the plants with this package had runs that were on schedule. In contrast, those that were organized along more traditional lines, using none of these inclusion-inducing management approaches, performed much more poorly. Only 88 percent of their runs were "on schedule."[1]

Other investigations, examining conditions affecting the success of manufacturing in automobile plants, have also discovered that management of the three Rs produces measurable effects on organization performance.

Using both production time and defects-per-vehicle as measures of success, these studies report that automobile manufacturing plants characterized by pay-for-performance, lots of training opportunities, a focus on teams as the core work units, and quality control procedures in the hands of line workers took 22 hours to produce a vehicle with .5 defects. Other plants, working with more traditional, top-down, command and control arrangements, took 30 hours to produce the equivalent vehicle with .8 defects.[2]

Outcomes like these have direct effects on company profits and stockholders' benefits. When price-to-book valuation ratios, shareholder returns, and returns on capital were compared in studies including more than 700 companies, the results regularly favored those companies that managed the three **R**s in ways that sent messages of inclusion to employees.[3]

Malden Mills of Lawrence, Massachusetts, manufactures fabric. The firm's CEO, Mr. Aaron Feuerstein, has been praised as a saint and castigated as a fool. He earned this oddly contradictory reputation when he continued to give 1,000 employees their full pay for several months, while repairs occurred, after a fire destroyed his factory and their jobs.

Thomas Teal, a writer for *Fortune* magazine who spent time with Mr. Feuerstein, concluded that this CEO deserves neither adulation nor condemnation. Teal asks, "Why in the world should it be a sign of divinely inspired nuttiness to treat the workforce as if it was an asset, to cultivate the loyalty of employees who hold the key to recovery and success, to take risks for the sake of a larger future income stream, even to seek positive publicity?"[4]

Mr. Feuerstein is a businessperson. He is not a saint, nor is he a fool. When it is necessary, Aaron Feuerstein is perfectly able to tread paths that are unpopular with employees. Dismissals, for example, are not off his list of management's options. But he also recognizes that even when those choices are necessary, behaving in ways that crush the workforce's spirit is counterproductive to business success. Under Mr. Feuerstein's balanced stewardship, Malden Mills has had a 95 percent employee retention rate and, between 1982 and 1995, the company's revenues tripled without suffering commensurate increases in personnel costs.

Several years after the fire, Malden Mills faced a financial crisis. It owed $140 million. Proper management of the three **R**s of organizational life does not exempt firms from the cost of business errors, and some contend that Malden Mills erred by underestimating foreign competition and overestimating the sales potential of certain products. Boston University's School of Management Professor David Weil disagrees, arguing that the company could not have anticipated problems created by a declining economy and competitor products.

There might be uncertainty about whether errors were made, but there is no uncertainty about the degree to which Feuerstein's earlier efforts yielded a broad sense of *we*. "Much-loved Malden Mills has plenty of admirers. Local residents have organized a Web-based 'Buy Fleece' campaign…. Townspeople recently sent checks… a token of support" and two Massachusetts Senators, Edward M. Kennedy and John Kerry, have urged the firm's creditors not to force it to file for bankruptcy.[5] Sentiment like this does not have a price tag.

Bosses can buy technology. Conformity, compliance, and obedience can even be for sale. But no amount of money purchases employees' commitment or loyalty. Cash cannot be exchanged for their initiative, creativity, or the efforts that continue to occur even when bosses are not watching. Those work behaviors depend on inclusion, identity, and the psychological golden rule of organizations. They require proper management of the three **R**s of organization life.

Managing the Three Rs: Rewards

Year-to-year increases in executive compensation should be conspicuously tied to company performance. The indices and algebra for calculating performance and calibrating it to compensation should be publicly announced at the outset of a salary year and remain unmodified during that entire period.

There is no one way to define a point at which executive compensation becomes *too much*. Two contemporary business heroes, Jack Welch and Lou Gerstner, former CEOs of General Electric and IBM, respectively, have added immensely to their companies' market values. For those accomplishments they deserve substantial rewards. But the rewards that they or any bosses receive will send more powerful messages of inclusion to their workforces when they are, first, transparently calibrated to organization performance, and second, linked to formulas used for compensating the remainder of the workforce. Calibration and linkage build *we*-group ties by signifying that organization successes and failures are the consequences of interdependent efforts of employees from the hierarchy's bottom to its top.

End repricing and gross-ups. Financial schemes such as repricing options and gross-ups invariably create inequities by providing exclusive compensation privileges to an elite. Current accounting rules fail to do what is necessary. They require companies to take a charge against earnings when more than one-third of their outstanding options are repriced.[6] Instead of ending repricing, those rules might merely encourage organizational decision makers to keep the number of options that they do reprice below the one-third threshold.

Isolate managements' personal contributions to their organizations' successes from general stock market oscillations. In some companies— for example, Royal Dutch/Shell and BT (British Telecom)[7]—that isolation is established by indexing the rise and fall of a company's stock price to rises and falls in the S&P. This adjustment prevents extreme fluctuations in the overall market from either hurting or helping option recipients.

Narrow the currently increasing compensation gap between personnel at organizations' tops and bottoms. Starbucks Corporation moves toward narrowing the compensation gap by providing all employees, including part-timers, with health insurance, stock options, training, and career counseling. The payoff for Starbucks has been a turnover rate that is less than 60 percent annually in an industry that has suffered from a 300 percent rate of turnover.[8]

Sometimes, instead of narrowing the gap between *they* and *we*, companies' compensation practices cause it to expand. The consequences can be dire. When 6,200 Northwest Airline pilots went on strike in August 1998, some attributed the acrimony that developed to events that occurred five years earlier.[9] In 1993, Alfred A. Cheechi and Gary L. Wilson purchased Northwest Airlines in a leveraged buyout involving a $20 million investment and a $3.1 billion debt. Soon afterward, when the airline's revenues tumbled, financial disaster was averted because pilots agreed to $900 million in wage concessions. Reports indicate that both Northwest Airlines and its employees' unions heralded the occasion as the beginning of a new era of cooperation.

If there ever was such a new era, then it appears to have ended abruptly in 1996 when the company refused to give pilots a 3 percent pay raise that they felt they were due. Their claim was based on calculations stemming from the 1993 agreement that linked Northwest pilots' pay to pilots' pay at four competing airlines. Making matters worse was the widening gap between the pay that these employees were being offered and senior management's rewards.

Northwest Airline profits in 1996 and 1997 reached record levels. Northwest executives and directors used the opportunity to reap large financial benefits. In early 1998, Gary L. Wilson reportedly sold 300,000 shares of stock for $15.2 million, and the company's CEO, John Dasburg, received $19 million when he cashed in his options.

The pilots eventually won their claim in arbitration, but their feelings of being wronged by what they saw as the company's effort to renege on a promise that would have narrowed the income gap evidently continued unabated. Referring to the incident, a spokesperson for the pilots is quoted as saying, "That broke the partnership bond.... You can track the decline in morale and service back to that."[10]

Although no specific threshold can be identified, there is surely a crossover point after which the size of the compensation gap causes a great number of employees to believe that their employing organizations are hostile alien entities being run by bosses for *their* benefit, not *ours*. The result, inside organizations and in society at large, is alienation from business organizations and the powerful privileged boss elites who appear to control them.

Link nonexecutive employee compensation to organization performance. Tying nonexecutive employee compensation to organization performance creates a basis for transforming self-interest into a sense of ownership with positive effects on a workforce's attitudes and productivity, as well as company profits.[11] There is convincing evidence that linking compensation and performance has benefit when the compensation is large enough and there is a clear line-of-sight between employees' work efforts and organization performance.[12] Sadly, despite all the supporting empirical and anecdotal evidence, data published in 1998 reveal that only 10 million U.S. employees (far less than 10 percent of the workforce) worked in firms that provide ESOPs (Employee Stock Option Plans), a major scheme for linking employee compensation to their companies' performance.[13]

Sharing performance gains with employees also might increase their willingness to invent ways of raising productivity. The resulting innovations sometimes make it possible to increase salary without increasing product prices. For example, by successfully introducing new equipment, Sonoco Products was able to increase production of plastic bags from 450 to 750 per minute. The cost advantage that increase provided allowed wage raises without offsetting price hikes. And Goodman Equipment Corporation, based in Bedford Park, Illinois, was able to introduce ways of cutting labor costs incurred during the production of locomotives that it sells to mining companies. Without adding to product prices, those savings in labor costs permitted salary and benefit costs to grow to 22 percent of sales from 20 percent. Innovations like these are unlikely to be generated by employees who expect that the resulting gains will be reflected in bosses' compensation, but not in their own paychecks.[14]

What works at a hierarchy's bottom also works at its top. Organization benefits are sometimes realized when compensation for members of the Board of Directors is linked to organization performance. It is an argument for requiring directors to take nontrivial equity positions in companies where they are board members. Sunbeam board member Professor Charles M. Elsom illustrates the point. When he joined the company's Board of Directors in 1996, Mr. Elsom was reported to have purchased $100,000 of Sunbeam stock. At first, that investment rose in value, to $250,000, then it fell 80 percent, to $50,000, during the time that Alfred J. Dunlap was Sunbeam's CEO. It hardly takes imagination to believe that Professor Elsom's losses were a wake-up call. He was the one who brought a motion to the board asking for Mr. Dunlap's removal as Sunbeam's CEO.[15]

Reward systems that tie individual compensation only to individual performance often have effects that are contrary to company interests and opposite to those that occur when reward systems link individual compensation to either team or organization performance. Those using only individual performance as the basis for calculating individual compensation can cause competitive, impersonal, narrowly task-oriented work relationships. In contrast, those that connect employees' compensation to the performance of either their work teams or the entire organization have a greater chance of producing work relationships characterized by cooperation, closeness, and solidarity. Connections like those expand the boundaries of *we*, while those that disconnect individual compensation from others' performance, promote self-interest, shrinking *we* until all that is left is *me, me, and me*!

Workers, herded into war with one another by organization reward systems that encourage competition are compelled to compare their work to that of competitors—that is, other employees—instead of recognizing its contribution to organizational goal achievement. The reason is entirely understandable: In the minds of workers who are forced to compete for scarce rewards, survival requires excelling in comparison to their coworkers. That win-lose goal has at least two consequences: It tends to motivate individual performance that is self-serving, with little regard for its effects on the whole, and it stirs up plots to undermine others' performance using Machiavellian tactics such as withholding information and playing office politics.

In competitive work settings, self-centered work behavior increases because, from employees' perspectives, it hardly matters whether their own performance improves, or the performance of other employees deteriorates. Employees seeking protection and victory only need to outdo coworkers, who have become their *de facto* competitors. Unfortunately, as employees individually strive for protection and victory, their combined behaviors swell into a competitive frenzy. Over time, as the spiraling competition occupies larger portions of each employee's workday behavior, *we* diminishes and *I* grows, until only self-interest remains.

Managing the Three Rs: Respect

Attend to employees as people, not just as workers.

USAA, a San Antonio-based company that is largely managed by former military officers, sells insurance to military officers. Experts might predict that the company's targeted customer market is a difficult one in which to grow a business because the United States armed forces is a limited market. If they were to make that prediction, then they would not be able to use USAA's growth in revenues and profits to support their pessimistic prognosis. USAA's business has grown because satisfied customers keep coming back for more of the expanding product services that the company offers.

After studying the company, one observer concluded, "What makes USAA's growth recipe work isn't just the ingredients. It's the execution." He then added, "USAA makes it easy for its employees to work hard. Its campus-like setting boasts restaurants, convenience stores, fitness centers, playing fields, a child care center, a dry cleaner, and a post office." Most USAA employees work 4-day, 38-hour weeks, travel in company vans, and are eligible for some of the $2.7 million in funds for college tuition reimbursement provided by the company.[16]

Raul Navarez, a security guard at USAA, succinctly explained why all this attention to the whole person works. He said, "The facilities say that the company cares about us, that we're a valued asset."[17]

The effects of USAA's concern for employees' commitment and loyalty was not lost on the company's CEO, Robert Herres, when, in 1996, he was quoted as saying, "It's hard to convince the workforce that this growth opportunity is for real, that there are job opportunities here, that there won't be pink slips. They've read so much about downsizing, and they think it will happen here. I tell them the only limitation to growth is how well we do our jobs." (Note the use of *we* and *our* rather than *you* or *your*.)

First Tennessee National Bank is also a company where it is recognized that the leadership of business requires attention to employees as people, not simply workers. Ralph Horn, the Bank's CEO, linked customer service and motivated employees, saying, "The two are tied to a point where they really can't be separated." A vice president of loan operations at the Bank, Ms. Tina Williford, reported that in five years the volume of work done by her 88-person division doubled, while its customer ratings moved to a remarkable 98 percent favorable, from a pitiful 38 percent favorable. She attributed these gains to the way employees are treated: "Flextime," "flexplace," and employee involvement are central to the organization's functioning. The company cares about the whole person.[18]

Hewitt Associates' consultant Ray Baumruk had similar things to say about customer service after his experiences with a customer services unit of a credit card processing firm. Results of a survey showed that employees in the unit did not feel valued. Subsequently, "The company provided private workspaces, created work teams, and started training and selecting managers with greater care. Turnover fell to about 15 percent from about 35 percent to 40 percent."[19]

In 1998, SAS Institute was an $850 million producer of statistical software located near Raleigh, North Carolina. The company's CEO was James H. Goodnight, Ph.D., who once confessed that he likes "happy people." In order to make them happy people, Dr. Goodnight provided employees with a free health clinic, two day care centers, flextime based on a 35-hour week, a subsidized cafeteria with its own pianist, year-end bonuses, and profit sharing. There were also discounts available for home purchases, club memberships, and airfares. There was a company choir, a specialist to help select ergonomically beneficial furniture, and free snacks. The result was an industry low 4 percent rate of turnover and enormous recruitment appeal.

It would be an error to use Dr. Goodnight's attention to his employees as people to stereotype him as a "goody-two shoes" softy in executive's clothing. Dr. Goodnight listens to employees but maintains his authority over business matters. He decides what products will be brought to market. He draws draft designs of the company's future work facilities, determines sites for new buildings, and even maintains veto power over artwork.[20]

Matsushita, one of the dramatic business stories of the twentieth century, is also a company where the presence of a strong leader has not altered the decisive role that concern for the whole employee plays in creating business success.

During the early years of the Depression, managers at a company producing Matsushita electric appliances concluded that survival depended on laying off as much as 50 percent of the workforce. The company's founder, Konsuke Matsushita, had other ideas. He kept every employee, eliminated holidays, and cut both production and the length of the workday. Wages were untouched, but employees were asked to make special efforts to sell existing inventory. The result was cheers, effort, and rapid inventory reduction. Regular work shifts were quickly re-established and the company moved into new product areas. In the decades that followed, Matsushita grew into a company with the equivalent of tens of billions of dollars in annual revenue and a workforce in the tens of thousands. A cornerstone of the company's managerial policy has always been a concern for employees and the communities in which they live.[21]

John P. Kotter, a leading authority on Matsushita, concluded that, because of the founder's leadership, hallmarked by a broad-ranging concern for employees, the workforce became a competitive advantage "despite ever-increasing size and the general tendency for corporations to lose employee commitment over time."[22]

See employees in terms of their future employability as well as their current employment. Jack Welch, General Electric's former CEO, put this issue front-and-center in a statement that he made about what companies must give employees in order to get their loyalty. *My concept of loyalty is not 'giving time' to some corporate entity and, in turn, being shielded and protected from the outside world. Loyalty is an affinity among people who want to grapple with the outside world and win.... The new psychological contract is that jobs at GE are the best in the world for people who are willing to compete. We have the best training and development resources and an environment committed to providing opportunities for personal and professional growth.*[23]

Some years ago, when NYNEX was the New York and New England regional telephone company, it developed revolutionary ways of creating "the best training and development resources and an environment committed to providing opportunities for personal and professional growth." The innovation began with a crisis. The company was faced with the prospect of reducing its 35,000-person workforce by 8,000 jobs, about 23 percent.[24] Job automation and a loss of customers to new competitors were among the crisis' major causes. In response, NYNEX developed an agreement with one of its largest unions, the Communication Workers of America (CWA), allowing the company to achieve necessary business goals without using involuntary layoffs. Instead of firing employees, NYNEX increased early retirement and voluntary severance incentives, instituted job sharing, brought back outsourced work, and reduced its use of temporary employees. Most importantly, with respect to employability, the company established the NYNEX Next Step Program and NYNEX University.

Joining the program was touted to be a return to school, homework, exams, and studying. It was going to be hard work, but employees were eager to do it. Several thousand of them immediately expressed interest in joining this program that was only prepared to enroll 1,000 participants each year. Employees accepted into the program worked four days and went to school on the fifth. NYNEX paid their salary and tuition, and supplied each one of them with a laptop computer. After two years, employees who successfully completed the program had up-to-date, practical knowledge about the world of telecommunications. They received an Associate Degree in Applied Science and additional wages. Some could also leave the company for two years in order to work on a four-year college degree. Once that degree was earned, they were free to return to the company with a guarantee of undiminished benefits and seniority. One evaluation of the program maintained, "The people who have helped build this company now have the opportunity to take it to its next level." The speaker was a union man, William G. Casey, CWA co-director of the Next Step Program.[25] His statement shows how, by introducing this program, NYNEX was saying to its workforce *We're in this together, you're not simply an expendable commodity.*

Make a genuine effort to maintain employability, not an ironclad guarantee of employment. Ted Castle's experience as CEO of Rhino Foods, a Vermont dessert manufacturer, illustrates the point.

Several years ago, when Rhino Foods' production capacity exceeded consumer demand, instead of dismissing one-third of the firm's employees, Ted Castle involved them in a search for ways of effectively using excess staff. Eventually, some of Rhino's employees were temporarily placed with one of the company's biggest customers. As a practical matter, the experience of working for that customer provided employees with skills that were useful to Rhino Foods. But the process Rhino Foods used in order to achieve that gain is equally important. CEO Castle said, *Asking my employees for solutions not only solved a difficult problem, but engendered loyalty and built trust among the staff.*[26]

Don't expect we to be everyone. Bosses' efforts at inclusion, however genuine they might be, will not be accepted by 100 percent of the workforce. Personal disposition, past experiences, and self-interest impede the success of inclusion-inducing management approaches. Employees typically see themselves as disadvantaged with respect to evaluations of performance, authority to act, and recognition of their contributions.[27] Some bosses use these self-perceptions as justification for ignoring the legitimate needs and concerns of all their employees, defending their arrogant indifference by claiming that *they will not be grateful anyway.* These bosses are drawing the wrong conclusion by using the actions of some employees to condemn the whole workforce. Moreover, even when a number of employees actually mistrust bosses' inclusive efforts, any expression of indifference on bosses' parts only worsens whatever employee reluctance already exists.

Although persistence in the face of employee withdrawal is essential, because *we* will never be the entire workforce, it is important to recognize that disagreements do not disappear simply because the boss' grit eventually gets the process right. Disputes about real issues create real divisions among people who work in organizations. Evidently, that is what happened at GM's Saturn plant in Spring Hill, Tennessee.

Sales of Saturn cars peaked in the 1980s, but then fell 20 percent between 1993 and 1997 because of higher gasoline prices and the entrance of competitively priced cars made by Asian manufacturers. Layoff fears at Saturn mounted, and in 1997, bonuses fell to $2,200, from $10,000 in the previous two years. In the midst of all this difficulty, a vote was scheduled in which 7,200 plant workers were going to decide about continuing one of the United States' most innovative labor contracts. Seventy-five pages long, this contract required cooperation between management and hourly workers. It provided workers with lower base pay but greater opportunity for earning bonuses linked to organization performance. The arrangement worked pretty well for a large majority of the workforce: Immediately before the vote, Saturn workers' base pay was reportedly between $36,774 and $41,787, with average annual yearly bonuses over a six-year period of more than $5,000. During the same time period, comparable assembly line workers elsewhere earned a base of about $40,622 and yearly bonuses of only $400.[28]

When the vote was counted, approximately two-thirds of the unionized workforce had voted to keep the contract. Michael E. Bennet, head of Local 1853 of the United Automobile Workers union, summarized the outcome saying, "The vote represents the fact that this local union membership is as dedicated and committed to the original Saturn idea as it was in 1985."[29]

Critics countered that one-third of the workforce voted "No," claiming it as evidence for the argument that cooperation does not work. They too are overgeneralizing and drawing the wrong conclusion. Even when the three **R**s of organization life are properly managed, real differences affecting self-interest will cause disagreements to occur, possibly as frequently as they do when the three **R**s are *improperly* managed. But the character of those disagreements and the way they are handled are likely to be very different.

When the three **R**s are properly managed, organization members identify one another as part of *we*, not as opposing members of *they* and *we*. What separates them is an issue, not an unbridgeable gap. Thus, the presence of *we*-group ties is capable of reducing dysfunctional escalation of conflict while increasing the possibility of mutually beneficial problem solving. It happens between allies and among the members of close-knit families all the time. Human fears and frailty do not automatically disappear when organizations properly manage the three **R**s of organization life; they are simply less likely to become the causes of destructive disagreements.

Make the leadership of business be about business. In 1992, a group of Eastern Airlines pilots pooled efforts and investments in order to form the now defunct Kiwi Air Lines. Guided by democratic zeal, in 1995, three years after the company's launching, its 1,000 employees flew airplanes to 61 cities, while receiving top ratings in quality surveys. In February of that same year, Kiwi Air Lines Chairman and founder Robert W. Iverson (Rocky) was dismissed.

Some mistakenly argue that the company's inclusive managerial approaches were responsible for Kiwi's problems and Mr. Iverson's dismissal. There are reports that some of Kiwi's employees, feeling too much like owners, ignored company decisions, refused to handle flights that they disliked, failed to make flight announcements, and gave away company resources to charity without authorization. Certainly, if any one of these abuses occurred, remedial measures were required. But it is an error to place the blame for this delinquency on inclusive management approaches. Every organization houses some employees who are malingerers and screw-ups. Kiwi seems not to have had more than its share of these "bad apples."

The fact is that other evidence makes it absolutely clear that most of Kiwi's employees were unusually committed to their company's success. On their own volition they cleaned aircraft, decorated them, and took pay cuts in order to thwart competitors. Personnel at Kiwi were described as "People with a selfless sense of mission.... *(who saw)* solutions not visible through the traditional clouds of adversarial corporate storminess."[30]

What then caused Kiwi's problems and Rocky Iverson's dismissal? The explanation for both probably begins in October 1994. It was then that Mr. Iverson, "By his own admission, ... mis-stepped by moving to put some…recommendations into effect…" before anyone could consider or comment on a critical report in which they were contained. Then, in December 1994, a deal that he worked out to raise cash was turned down when "…some directors criticized him for working behind their backs." In effect, in neither of these instances was Rocky Iverson acting in inclusive ways. On the contrary, his own observation, confirming the conclusion that he was behaving in exclusionary ways, was "I didn't spend enough time figuring out what was emotionally important to the rest of the people."

The difficulties caused by Rocky Iverson's behavioral errors were apparently compounded when Kiwi Air Line's zeal for the benefits of inclusion put it in a position from which it was unable to draw on the business acumen that it needed. Byron Hogue, a former Federal Express executive who took charge of Kiwi when Rocky Iverson left, explained that some of Kiwi's problems arose because a number of the pilots running the company lacked business experience. Kiwi pilots, in turn, were reportedly pointing their fingers at Mr. Iverson, saying that he did not have what was required to take the company beyond its entrepreneurial stage.[31]

The obviousness of the conclusion supported by these events at Kiwi in no way diminishes its importance: The indisputable benefits of having employees involved should not lead anyone to conclude that workforce will replaces business skill. Inclusion has important effects on employees' organizational identification, commitment, and loyalty, but successful organization performance requires the presence of business ability as well as employee motivation. In addition to Mr. Iverson's behavioral errors, Kiwi's failure evidently also occurred because the organization simply did not access essential business knowledge. If these were the principal causes of the company's failure, then it is regrettable, because what happened to Kiwi was probably avoidable. But the airline's failure should also serve as a potent reminder that the leadership of business is about business, even if it is not only about business.

Remember that leaders are we. *Rulers are* they. Bosses find their own ways of becoming one of *us* rather than one of *them* in the eyes of their employees. Robert Shillman, for example, CEO of Cognex, a company that produces software to monitor assembly line quality and was once ranked number 52 in *Fortune*'s list of fastest growing companies, appears to be a competent clown. He does a Three Stooges' routine for new hires, leads in singing a corporate anthem assisted by a rock band, and tosses moneybag bonuses from a Brink's truck. Mr. Shillman reasons, "Our antics break down barriers between managers and workers."[32]

Herb Kelleher, former CEO of Southwest Airlines, had his own means of breaking down barriers in order to broaden the boundaries of *we*. When he was with employees, apparently what you saw was what you got. Mr. Kelleher smoked, drank a good amount of Wild Turkey (that's an alcoholic beverage), did rap music, and arm-wrestled. By all accounts, employees seemed to enjoy his down-to-earth authenticity and, as members of the same organization, he and they enjoyed the company's very successful growth. [33]

Some have identified Southwest as "the most successful airline in history."[34] During 2001, the firm's market capitalization was $14 billion, more than American, United, and Continental combined. In that year's first quarter, when other airlines were losing money due, in part, to rising fuel costs, Southwest made $121 million in net profits; 65 percent more than the year before.

What contributed to Kelleher's success as a boss? He was a leader, not a ruler. He explained it by saying, "You have to treat your employees like customers. When you treat them right, then they will treat your outside customers right. That has been a powerful competitive weapon for us. You have to take the time to listen to people's ideas. If you just tell somebody no, that's an act of power ... an abuse of power." Kelleher confessed that he learned these leadership principles from his mother. "She said that positions and titles signify absolutely nothing. They're just adornments; they don't represent the substance of anybody."[35]

One of Mr. Kelleher's characteristics, accessibility, is a quality also attributed to Mary Kay (Ash) of Mary Kay, Inc. fame. In addition to her day-to-day availability, before her stroke in 1996, she apparently invited employees to her home for tea several times a year. One of them, Janice Byrd, who worked at Mary Kay, Inc.'s Dallas headquarters, spoke about how Ms. Kay's efforts at inclusion affected both individual employees and the company's work culture. She said that employees "...increased their own self-esteem by being around her, and they want to pass that on to others the same way she did."[36]

Despite their personal quirks, or perhaps precisely because they were good-humoredly willing to display them, business leaders like Shillman, Kelleher, and Kay have contributed to building bonds of *we* between their employees and their organizations. These leaders did not hide themselves behind the off-putting facade of royal reserve. Similar displays of bosses' feelings, even when they are sad, also have inclusive effects on the work force.

Folks need to grieve when a loved one has died. Each year, approximately 4,000,000 workers suffer such a loss. Despite these huge numbers, unofficial organization policies often let the bereaved know "that's *your* problem, not *ours*," providing them with no support and little or no room to grieve. Bosses, taking a cue from the unwritten policy, frequently act as if workforce respect comes from "playing it close to the vest" and being stoically unemotional no matter what the pain. The experience of Bill Foote proves them wrong.

Mr. Foote was CEO of USG, a Chicago-based building products firm. At the time of his wife's death, in 1997, the company had $2.59 billion in sales. Although he had not held the job for very long, Mr. Foote decided to speak with his staff about her death, his grieving, and some of the tragedy's implications for how he would be managing his relationships with the company in the near future. Since Bill Foote is generally regarded as someone who does not go around sharing deep emotions, it is likely that he did not approach this conversation as if it were just another appearance before the troops.

What he did mattered. Coworkers are reported as saying that "They're wasn't a person in the room who didn't think 'Here's a helluva guy.'" The explicit message from them was "If we have to go through a few walls for this guy, we're going to do it."[37] Mr. Foote's display of human vulnerability produced connection, not pity. He opened up and was invited in.

Peter Luchetti, who was global head of project finance at Bank of America (San Francisco), in 1998, observed, "People are left feeling empty at work if you don't provide some sort of bonding experience."[38] So, in order to create that experience, he had employees join him in a kitchen where they worked as a team preparing ice cream and Italian food. Bosses at Genentech Inc., PG&E Corp., and Wells Fargo Bank have done the same. They are part of a growing list of companies that have gathered employees around hot stoves in order to break down barriers and build connections.

Forget the particulars. Precise mimicry of Shillman, Kelleher, Kay, Foote, or Luchetti, is not essential. Focus on the principle, not the practice. It is necessary to send employees messages of inclusion that disavow elitism. How that happens can vary considerably from boss to boss. Abuse does not work, and stereotypical, stylized royal responses do not seem to send the correct messages either. But by no means is it necessary to act like a clown. That was simply one person's way of expressing the principle. It works for him. Find your equivalent.

Managing the Three Rs: Recognition

Syncrude Canada Ltd. has been the "world's leading producer of light, sweet crude oil from oil sand." In addition to having this major position in the petrochemicals industry, the company has also operated a utility plant, a bitumen extraction plant, and facilities for processing bitumen. All together, these operations have provided work for approximately 15,000 Canadians.

Syncrude Ltd. also deserves credit for perfecting an approach to management in which the voices of all employees, from the hierarchy's top to its bottom, play a key role in producing financial success. The company calls its management innovation "Participative Redesign." In a widely distributed company document, Syncrude Ltd. explains that this managerial approach "affirms each individual's right to be involved in decisions which affect them at work and, further, it is only through full and energetic participation of the majority that work can be successfully reconstructed." Then, defying elites everywhere, Syncrude's statement's closing refrain declares *"redesign is not a matter for experts."*[39]

A quick reading of this statement might lead you to think that "participative redesign" authorizes organization anarchy. No conclusion could be further from the truth. Syncrude understands that employee voice, supported through company-supplied information and autonomy, also needs company-supplied direction. Hence, employees' participative redesign efforts are guided by a series of Syncrude Ltd. principles:

Changes in organization structures and processes must be aligned with the values and vision to which the company is committed.

In their efforts to use "continuous improvement" processes in order to maintain Syncrude's expressed standards of safety, reliability, and productivity, the company insists that managers and supervisors encourage their teams to develop and use reliable statistical tools.

Instead of chunking tasks in order to facilitate top-down surveillance, teams are given responsibility for whole tasks or, if that is not possible, then they are given an understanding of where their tasks fit into the whole.

In order to maintain a business/product focus in work teams, Syncrude Ltd. promises to build support services into work teams, but where that is not possible the company promises that the services will be made readily accessible within the same business unit. (In practice, this means crossing team and department boundaries in order to work together and take joint responsibility for continuously improving safety, reliability, productivity, and the quality of working life.) Syncrude Ltd. believes that "...we need organization structures and processes that encourage, in fact, require the continuous flow of information, skills and resources throughout our operations."

Further, the company explicitly places customer focus ahead of internal focus. Restating the principle that work should be designed in such a way that each person clearly identifies with the whole task, Syncrude Ltd. asserts that in order to "express this principle, each work unit's objective must be to deliver the product or service according to customers' specifications. This will require getting close to the customer in order to continuously improve information sharing and understanding."

Giving employees the opportunity to alter existing rules is regarded as being important as giving them opportunity to erect them in the first place. The Syncrude Ltd. list of principles concludes by stating that, "...the process of ongoing participative redesign never ends. We will continuously reconstruct work as we continue to discover new and better ways of working together." This statement's message of inclusion is clear. It invites employee voice by acknowledging that the firm's guiding principles are not the unquestionable decrees of infallible bosses.

Proof of the company's success in using "participative redesign" is in its production statistics. Between 1989 and 1995, Syncrude's annual crude oil production grew to 73.9 million barrels from only 54 million barrels, a gain of 37 percent. During that same six-year period, operating costs fell 20 percent, workforce size declined 23 percent, and employee productivity surged an extraordinary 71 percent.

Build work structures that enhance employees' opportunities to exercise voice. During 1994, Chrysler enjoyed a 246 percent run-up in earnings and a 20 percent upward move in sales. When Bob Eaton, Chrysler's CEO at the time, analyzed these gains, he attributed them to the formation of a "self-contained, multi-disciplinary group."

Mr. Eaton was referring to a group composed of approximately 700 Chrysler employees representing an array of different functions. The group's work began with senior management presenting its vision of a future vehicle, along with a set of tough goals for the vehicle's appearance, performance, and economy. "Then," said Mr. Eaton, "the 700 were freed to go to work, with each subgroup forming an organization that it felt was appropriate to the particulars of its task." He explained that there were no committees and no hierarchy outside the group. *"When decisions are made, they are made by somebody down in the organization who knows a helluva lot more about the issue than I do."* Despite the regrettable exclusion of blue-collar workers, according to Bob Eaton, the result of giving voice to these 700 Chrysler employees were cars designed below target for both total investment and cost-per-car.[40]

Design training to increase employee voice. Jacques Nasser, former CEO of another automobile manufacturer, Ford, changed the concept of training in order to raise employees' initiative, creativity, and commitment and diminish their perfunctory, obedient, going-through-the-motions work behavior. Working with University of Michigan Professor Noel Tichy, in 1997 Mr. Nasser introduced Ford managers to the Business Leadership Initiative (BLI) program. This is not a traditional program featuring classroom lectures. Participants' active voice about issues, not their passive ingestion of bosses' ideas, is the program's hallmark.

The BLI program involved 55,000 bosses at Ford in 100-day projects in which they work to solve real problems in real time while receiving timely, targeted inputs that provide opportunities for them to examine and modify the character and quality of their work behavior. The results of this self-directed, real-problems-in real-time training have been impressive. One group, working at a Wayne, Michigan Escort plant, for example, developed a means of washing Kevlar gloves that workers use when they have to handle sheet metal and glass. The washing meant that the gloves could be worn more than once, resulting in a savings of $115,000 a year, or 50 cents a car.[41]

BLI's message is affirming and respectful. "You can do it," it says. "Organization problem solving is not the special preserve of an elite." It is a matter of *we*, not *they*.

Having teams of employees who are in BLI training also work on a project for the community moves the *we*-group boundary still further. The projects that Ford's bosses worked on have included painting and landscaping public facilities, and restoring parkland. Efforts like those move the boundary of *we* so that it includes both the community and the organization icons. Bound by these ties, employees are less apt to look at either the community or the organization and think, "I'll worry about *me*, and let *them* worry about *them*."

Raise employees' voices to lower the difficulty of completing successful mergers and acquisitions. Many companies play the mergers/ acquisitions game, but only a few are good at it. If we look just at those that are called "mega-deals"—deals valued at over $1 billion—there are often more than 100 per year. One study of 100 large deals made between 1994 and 1997 reported, however, that approximately 66 percent of them experienced losses one year after the deal was consummated. That pattern of results is typical. In fact, the record of success has been dismal enough to prompt a former head of Lehman Brothers, Warren

Hellman, to comment, *"So many mergers fail to deliver what they promise that there should be a presumption of failure. The burden of proof should be on showing that anything really good is likely to come out of one."*[42] Although senior managers often realize financial gain regardless of a deal's eventual success, the frequent failures hurt both stockholders and employees.

Deals fail for several reasons:

- Resources that are diverted in order to build one business area for the new organization often result in losses to successful core businesses, offsetting whatever gains might occur.

- Newly created opportunities arising from the merger/acquisition are insufficiently unique. Competitors, nullifying any gains, easily copy them.

- Mergers and acquisitions sometimes compel efforts that absorb resources, hindering the development of defenses against competitors' assaults.

- Redesigning organization charts by sorting their hanging boxes and rewriting job descriptions sometimes becomes a private, expert-led, paper-and-pencil substitute for the discussions that are necessary to build new affiliations among the employees who actually occupy jobs.

- Instead of being driven by a vision of an improved business future, many mergers are undertaken to develop a defense against current marketplace dangers.

In contrast, the merger of Smith-Kline Beckman with the British pharmaceutical company, Beecham, is widely regarded as a business success. According to reports, this merger met or exceeded all its business goals. During the merger period, sales grew at an 11 percent compounded rate, and both pre-tax earnings and earnings per share grew at a 13 percent compounded rate. R&D had 12 percent growth, while 15 percent of the merged company's 1993 sales' volume was attributable to new products.

Bob Bauman, Beecham's CEO, described how this success depended on shifting the two companies' orientations to the merger from, "Here are two old companies. We're going to bring them together and take the best of each, to 'We're going to create a totally new company that's able to compete in the future.'"[43] Mr. Bauman correctly framed the objective with an emphasis on creating *we* rather than *them* and *us*.

One of the typical procedures used in this merger had the heads of regional units in the two companies join their staffs in working together to design the new company for that region. The purpose of this joint effort was first to identify and align values, and later to compose corresponding leadership behaviors and performance measures for the newly designed organization. Thus, practice and principle for the new organization were not only consistent and driven by relevant performance feedback measures; the employees themselves formulated them all.

In the six years between 1994 and 2000, Cisco Systems reportedly acquired 51 companies, nearly half of them during the last century's final months and the new century's beginning. Defying the odds, most of these acquisitions have been judged "successful."[44]

Money helped: Cisco made deals that were financially advantageous to employees of acquired companies. It increased salaries, improved expense allowances, and maintained existing, better benefits, even when they were inconsistent with Cisco's. Ms. Mimi Gigoux, Cisco's acquisition expert, declared, *"My standard rule is, I'm going to keep those people whole."* But more than money has produced Cisco's successes in the acquisition game. Reports make it clear that Cisco's orientation, like Smith-Kline Beckman's, is to create one company, rather than cherry-pick the better parts of two old ones.

Columbia University Professor and organization consultant Warner Burke described his work with a group of seven senior bank executives who had participated in a merger and were about to enter a second, larger one. Burke asked them to identify lessons from their first merger experience that might assist their management of the one that was upcoming. They came up with several items:

- Have an explicit image of the benefits of having *one*, where there were previously two.

- Enable employees to understand that image so that they can formulate supporting action.

- Develop open, truthful communication, even for matters that might cause pain; for example, job reduction.

- Build informal relationships between the employees.

- Physically leave the merging units' work sites in order to complete some of the preparatory work in territory that none of the groups own.

- Keep a watch on the consistency between behavior and principles.

- Establish a uniform and unifying goal by focusing on customers.

These items boil down to the same principal that guided Smith-Kline Beckman and Cisco: redraw *we/they* boundaries by creating one company.[45]

The Delta Consulting Group Inc. (now part of William H. Mercer, Inc.), headed by David Nadler, had a number of experiences with mergers/acquisitions from which they drew some pertinent lessons: *Change management, after mergers, acquisitions, and organization break-ups, requires employee participation in re-contracting with employers, creating a new identity, and integrating business units that were previously unconnected. Further, an organization's chance for post-merger/acquisition success is also improved if employees' voices are heard during efforts to design new systems for rewards, appraisal, training, selection, and dispensing information in ways that support the new organization's priorities.* [46]

Remember that voice is not enough. In 1995, after three years with CEO Arthur C. Martinez at the helm, Sears once again became a major player in the retail game. Its stock price, which jumped 71 percent over the previous year, was way ahead of the S&P index of 32 retailers, which had moved up only 10.3 percent during the same period. And, during the 1995 Christmas season, when other retailers' sales' increases over the previous year hovered at zero, Sears' sales pushed ahead 9.2 percent.

CEO Martinez said that he believed that business targets (measured by operating margins, inventory turnover, and ratio of overhead to sales) were met because "These came out of the organization; they were not delivered as the goal." Barbara Lehman, a Sears' executive, added, "Our focus is to push ownership down and have people take responsibility."

But Sears did more than simply give employees voice. One observer who commented on what else happened to make voice work said, "The effort goes far beyond pep rallies. It includes discussion groups, training sessions, new job descriptions, new operating structures, and a new pay system—all intended to place decision making closer to the customer and make it customer friendly. And it involves employees, soliciting their ideas, letting them experiment and improve their skills as they reach for better performance." [47] It was not just about voice.

Between 1995 and 1997, a self-directed, 480-person workforce at one Lucent Technology factory performed so well that not a single delivery deadline was missed while costs remained low. Many things contributed to this success. Voice was interwoven into every one of them, but the factory's success cannot be attributed to voice alone.[48]

Selection. The plant chose personnel who were able to work on teams, and then provided them with the room that they needed to use their teamwork skills.

Leadership. Guidance about direction was not abandoned. Management established end goals. But the workforce was involved in developing paths to those goals. Work teams were always able to suggest ways of altering both the manufacturing process and product design.

Information. Sharing up-to-date information about the workflow in public settings gave employees the knowledge that they needed in order to follow plans and correct progress when it went awry.

Customer focus. Having employees in direct contact with their internal and external customers provided opportunities for both input and influence that kept their work on course.

Rewards. Compensation was aligned with the work culture's priorities. Annual bonuses, a sizeable 15 percent of annual salary in 1996, were based on individual and team performance in equal proportion.

The implication is clear: *No single magic bullet will rid organizations of all their ailments.* Changing only one aspect of an organization, even when that aspect is something as important as employee voice, will not produce organization success.

Not very long ago, "horizontal organization structure" was the latest cure-all tool for managers. It joined a long string of predecessor-panaceas that included TQM (total quality management), CI (continuous improvement), BPR (business process re-engineering), T-groups (training groups), MBO (management-by-objectives), and, way back, ZBB (zero-based-budgeting).

This time, as before, some organization gurus encouraged audiences to "Take heart: That rare thing, a consensus, is beginning to evolve around a model corporation for perhaps the next 50 years—the horizontal corporation."[49] This model organized employees into teams inside work units that formed around core processes (e.g., product development, account management, or retail outlet support, rather than functions like marketing or finance). The gurus advised that the customer's perspective was the best vantage point for spotting those core processes. And they promised that the pot of gold awaiting organizations that were fortunate enough to reach the rainbow's end of this exercise was a flatter, leaner firm. The exercise itself, they said, should involve scrutiny of core processes in order to determine facets and personnel that added value and those that did not, producing a rational basis for eliminating what was and wasn't useful.

These are all potentially worthwhile ideas but, like so many other management tools, in the imaginations of bosses desperate for help, their promise was exaggerated into perfection. For too many, the horizontal organization offered an orderly, rational means for re-fashioning their companies in ways that would lower costs and raise productivity. It only had to be installed just like any other bit of technology. That meant that their leadership of business could stay focused on *just business*. The critical issue was for them to determine *what* had to be installed. *How* it was done, their own motives, and their relationships with employees were all among a group of irrelevancies that could be safely shoved aside.

This is one way in which so many bosses hold a worthwhile idea in front of their eyes and then, blinded by its allure, run right into a brick wall of human dynamics. They forget that the long-term success of managerial tools often, possibly always, depends on the methods used to create change as much as it does on the changes' contents. The next chapter, *Bonds of* We *Barriers of* They: *Binding Fractures*, explains the human dynamics that make this so.

---

[1] Ichniowski, C. K., K. Shaw, G. Prennushi. "Effects of human resource management practices on productivity." *Mimeograph*, Columbia University (June 10, 1993).

[2] MacDuffie J. P., K. Krafci. "Integrating technology and human resources for high-performance manufacturing." In T. Kochan, M. Useem *Transforming Organizations* (New York: Oxford University Press, 1992): 210–220.

[3] Casio, W. F. "Guide to responsible restructuring." US Department of Labor. Office of the American Workplace, 1995.

[4] Teal, T. "Not a fool, not a saint." *Fortune* (November 11, 1996): 201–214.

[5] Browning, L. "Fire could not stop a mill, but debts might." *New York Times* (November 28, 2001): C1, C5.

[6] Leonhardt, D. "Technology share plunge hurting stock options." *New York Times* (April 19, 2000): C1, C14.

[7] DeAenlle, C. "A British solution: Weigh success against the markets." *New York Times* (April 7, 2002): Bu5.

[8] Hammonds, K. H., W. Zeller, K. Melcher. "Writing a new social contract." *Business Week* (March 11, 1996): 60–61.

[9] Zuckerman, L. "Vote of no confidence in Northwest strike." *New York Times* (September 6, 1998): 20.

[10] Ibid.

[11] Conte, M., A. Tannenbaum. "Employee ownership: A report." Presented to the Economic Development Administration, U.S. Department of Commerce. (Ann Arbor: University of Michigan Survey Research Center, 1978).

[12] Lawler, E. E. III. *Strategic Pay* (San Francisco, CA: Jossey-Bass Publishers, 1990).

[13] Kaufman, J. "Sharing the wealth." *Wall Street Journal* (April 4, 1998): R10.

[14] Schlesinger, J. M. "Gains in productivity, profits curb inflation despite pay increases." *Wall Street Journal* (May 21, 1997): A1, A8.

[15] Bryant, A. "Executive cash machine." *New York Times* (November 8, 1998): Bu1, Bu12; Bryant, A. "Slowing the money train." *New York Times* (November 8, 1998): Bu12.

[16] Henkoff, R. "Growing your company: Five ways to do it right." *Fortune* (November 25, 1996): 78–88.

[17] Lieber, R. B. "Why employees love these companies." *Fortune* (January 12, 1998): 72–74.

[18] Shellenbarger, S. "Investors seem attached to firms with happy employees." *Wall Street Journal* (March 19, 1997): B1.

[19] Shellenbarger, S. "Employers are finding it doesn't cost much to make staff happy." *Wall Street Journal* (November 19, 1997): B1.

[20] Shellhardt, T. D. "An idyllic workplace under a tycoon's thumb." *Wall Street Journal* (November 23, 1998): B1, B4.

[21] Kotter, J. P. "Matsushita." *Fortune* (March 31, 1997): 105–111.

[22] Ibid.

[23] Bartlett, C.A., S. Goshal. "Changing the role of top management: Beyond systems to people." *Harvard Business Review* (May–June, 1995): 132–142.

[24] Casio, W. F. "Guide to responsible restructuring." U.S. Department of Labor. Office of the American Workplace, 1995.

[25] NYNEX Next Step Program. (An undated company brochure).

[26] Carey, P. M. "6 sweet ways to keep your key players." *Your Company* (August/September 1996): 44–47.

[27] Ashforth, B. E., F. Mael. "Social identity theory and the organization." *Academy of Management Review* 14 (1989): 20–39.

[28] Meredith, R. "Many at Saturn auto factory are finding less to smile about." *New York Times* (March 6, 1998): A1, D2.

[29] Meredith, R. "Saturn union votes to retain its cooperative company pact." *New York Times* (March 12, 1998): D1, D4.

[30] Bryant, A. "One big happy family no more." *New York Times* (March 22, 1995): D1, D5.

[31] Ibid.

[32] "Smart managing," *Fortune* (March 31, 1997): 13.

[33] Lieber, R. B. "Why employees love these companies." *Fortune* (January 12, 1998): 72–74.

[34] Brooker, K. "The chairman of the board looks back." *Fortune* (May 28, 2001): 63–76.

[35] Ibid.

[36] Lieber, "Why employees love these companies," 74.

[37] Shellenberger, S. "A CEO opens up about loss and he finds he's a stronger boss." *Wall Street Journal* (September 10, 1997): B1.

[38] *Wall Street Journal* (November 24, 1998): A1.

[39] Memo: Principles for organizing work. *Syncrude* (October 8, 1993).

[40] Loeb, M. "Empowerment that pays off." *Fortune* (March 20, 1995): 145–146.

[41] Simison, R. L. "Ford rolls out new model of corporate culture." *Wall Street Journal* (January 13, 1999): B1, B4.

[42] Sirower, M. "What acquiring minds need to know." *Wall Street Journal* (February 22, 1999): A18.

[43] Burke, W. W. and W. Trahant. *Business Climate Shifts* (Woburn, MA: Butterworth Heinemann, 2000): 61.

[44] Thurm, S. "Under Cisco's system, mergers usually work; That defies the odds." *Wall Street Journal* (March 1, 2000): A1, A12.

[45] Burke, W.W. "The new agenda for organization development." *Organization Dynamics* (Summer, 1997): 1–14.

[46] Delta Consulting Group Inc. "Beyond the break-up." *Delta Insights* (1998).

[47] Dobrzynski, J. "Yes, he's revived Sears. But can he reinvent it?" *New York Times* (January 7, 1996): F1, F8–F9.

[48] Petzinger, T. "How Lynn Mercer manages a factory that manages itself." *Wall Street Journal* (March 3, 1997): B1.

[49] Jacobs, R. "The struggle to create an organization for the 21st century." *Fortune* (April 3, 1995): 90–96.

6

Bonds of We, Barriers of They: Binding Fractures

During the past quarter century, research evidence collected in localities as different as Brooklyn, New York and Bristol, England has proven that human beings possess few psychological forces as powerful as their ability to survey the surrounding social community and then mentally cleave it into a *we-group*, in which they include themselves, and one or more *they-groups*. Life provides nearly everyone with experiences that demonstrate the power of this division between the bonds of *we* and the barriers of *they*.

Promotive Tension

Bonds of *we* tie parents to their children, sports enthusiasts to favored teams, motion picture patrons to fictional characters, and patriots to beloved nations. Because these ties exist, children's problems keep parents awake at night, we weep, applaud, or cringe in movie theaters, defend *our* favorite teams, mourn their defeats[1], and sacrifice life and limb for *our* nation. By tying powerful feelings to what we imagine will be others' outcomes, bonds of *we* motivate us to advance others' goal attainment, just as barriers of *they* motivate us to hinder it.

Some of the most intriguing evidence about how *we*-group bonds affect human behavior in organizations was obtained in a dozen different investigations involving thousands of pedestrians walking along city streets.[2]

If you had been an unwitting participant in one of those investigations, your involvement would have begun when your ordinary, everyday walk along your local shopping street became a tiny bit more extraordinary in the instant that you came upon a stranger's lost wallet. After picking up the wallet (something that most pedestrians readily do, if investigators surreptitiously place the wallet on a litter-free street, near the curb, where passersby tend to look down before taking a step), you would probably rummage through its contents, discovering some money (an amount that varied between 2 and 10 U.S. dollars), as well as information about the person who lost the material.

At this point, a common question existed for both the participating pedestrians and the curious investigators: *Does the wallet (including the money) get returned to its rightful owner?* The answer largely depends on whether the stranger who "lost" it is linked to the finder by bonds of *we*, or separated from him or her by barriers of *they*.

Knowing some simple facts about the communities in which these investigations took place made it easy for the investigators to create bonds of *we* and barriers of *they*. Before any wallets were "lost," a survey of those communities identified opinions that were endorsed by nearly all their residents. When the time came to "lose" wallets, the investigators already knew which opinions were shared by more than 9 out of 10 pedestrians walking along the communities' central shopping streets. That knowledge about community opinion was used to create bonds of *we* or barriers of *they* in the following way: Information that pedestrians found with the wallets was systematically varied so that some of them learned that the stranger who "lost" the material shared their opinions on one or more issues, while others learned that the stranger's opinions differed from theirs.

When opinions agreed, and pedestrians were tied to the stranger through bonds of *we*, more than 80 percent of them returned the lost wallets (including *all* of the money). They did it anonymously, without any hope of future reward. If the stranger's opinion differed from the pedestrians', creating barriers of *they*, only a bit more than 20 percent of them returned the "lost" wallets. The explanation for this pattern, which has been observed repeatedly in different settings with various groups regardless of the amount of money contained in the wallet, involves a special form of empathy. It is called *promotive tension.*

Promotive tension occurs when relationships cause us to stand in another's shoes. It is then that our level of comfort is vulnerable to being either raised or lowered by expectations that we have about another's pleasure or plight. *Promotive tension* is what happens to parents, movie patrons, sports fans, and patriots.

Proving the point is research showing that members of *we* don't help one another willy-nilly, to the same degree on every occasion. *Promotive tension* among members of *we* appears to really put them into one another's shoes. Specifically, a series of controlled research investigations provided clear evidence that the rises and falls in the number of times *we*-group members helped the wallet's owner showed that they were behaving as if they felt the owner's sense of plight with some precision. (In contrast, when barriers of *they* separated these same people from the wallet's owner, they did not stand in that person's shoes, there was no promotive tension, no sense of the owner's plight, and, most importantly, almost no helping.) These investigations made use of a phenomenon that was first observed by investigators almost three-quarters of a century ago.

Behavioral scientists have known for a long time that the closer individuals are to completing a desired goal, the greater is their own urge to finish whatever tasks might remain in order to reach the objective. Whereas, when goal completion is more distant, although individuals might still intend to move forward, the urge is notably less strong. Everyday conversation contains lots of expressions that capture this phenomenon: *I was so close that I just had to get it done. It was so near that I could taste it. How could I stop with so little to go?* The typical behavior of airplane passengers provides additional evidence of the effect. On a six-hour flight, watch how their level of restlessness changes in the last 30 or 40 minutes of the journey. And on a one-hour flight, watch how the level rises during the trip's final 10 or 15 minutes. In behavioral sciences' jargon, this phenomenon is known as the *goal gradient effect.* Knowing the whys and wherefores of the effect's occurrence, once again, permitted investigators to collect evidence on city streets and in psychology laboratories in order to show the power of bonds of *we* and barriers of *they.*

In these investigations, after finding the "lost" material (a charity contribution, in this case), pedestrians learned about not only the stranger's opinion (establishing that person as part of either *we* or *they*), but also how *close* or *distant* the stranger was from completing his or her goal of making a set of 10 charitable contributions.

When pedestrians were tied to the stranger through bonds of *we,* and goal completion was near, it was as if finders empathically "felt" the stranger's more powerful urgings. *Promotive tension* heightened and approximately 80 percent of them returned what was lost. As the stranger's distance from goal completion increased, the level of urging that finders felt on the stranger's behalf decreased, promotive tension declined, and the percentage of returns dropped radically. When the contribution was only the second in the series of 10, for example, rates of return fell to a mere 20 percent, exactly what barriers of *they* produced no matter how close or distant the stranger was from completing the ultimate goal of 10 contributions.[3]

What this means is simple: When bonds of *we* existed, distance to the end-goal mattered. *Promotive tension* was aroused. The stranger's plight became the finders', and their helping appears calibrated to the levels of desire that would have been aroused in them if the lost contribution had been their own. When there were barriers of *they,* the stranger's plight was irrelevant to finders. *Promotive tension* was not aroused. Very little helping occurred, no matter how close or distant the stranger was from achieving goal completion. But all this is scientific background. It establishes the human dynamics through which *promotive tension* influences employees' work behavior.

Promotive tension is the emotional fuel that energizes the psychological golden rule of organizations: *Harming you becomes difficult for me because the two of us are part of* we. When workers' bonds of *we* include the employing organization, *promotive tension* causes news about organizational accomplishments to generate positive feelings, and news about organizational failures to generate negative ones. When these bonds are absent, there is no fuel to power the psychological golden rule of organizations. Consequently, just as when pedestrians who felt no connection to a stranger selfishly kept the lost material that they found, the work behavior of employees who possess no emotional attachment to employers is disproportionately influenced by calculations of self-interest. At the end of a day's work they leave without turning off the lights because it doesn't bother them one whit and they are not going to receive any tangible gain from making the extra effort.

Of course, even when they exist, the bonds of *we, promotive tension,* and the psychological golden rule of organizations never entirely eliminate self-interest as an influence on work behavior. But widely published empirical evidence shows that their presence in social relationships substantially diminishes the impact of self-interest. Some of the contributing investigations examined conditions that prompt group members to forgo self-serving choices in order to conserve community resources.[4]

A classic, hypothetical portrayal of the dilemma that conservation of community resources creates for individuals is contained in a story in which several ranchers' herds graze on common grassland. Since larger herds mean more income, it is in each rancher's financial interests to increase a herd's size. If each rancher acts only in self-interest, however, they are all endangered because the capacity of the grassland to support grazing is limited. If the herds grow too large, then the grassland will fail.

In this portrayal of the problem, the ranchers' decisions to maintain or expand their herds have readily observable consequences: The ranchers can easily keep a count of the number of animals in every other rancher's herd. When the consequences of delinquency are this obvious, it permits organizations to use social sanctions in order to constrain individual behavior that threatens to deplete their resources. When such surveillance is not possible, however, organizations must rely on individual self-restraint to prevent collective harm from occurring. Investigations of situations in which monitoring is imperfect show that positive emotional ties to social institutions are the strongest predictors of members' readiness to voluntarily restrain self-interest in favor of conserving community resources.

Even more remarkable is evidence that positive emotional attachment to social institutions enhances the occurrence of self-restraint in cases of domestic violence. Studies of domestic violence have shown that the likelihood of future spousal assault is affected more by a couple's perceptions of how fairly they have been treated by the "system" than by previous arrests or threats of future arrests.[5] It is not that the "system's" treatment of the couple discourages violence by causing their love to deepen. The way they are treated stems the occurrence of domestic violence by bonding them to a community that frowns on spousal abuse. Because the community becomes part of their *we*-group, promotive tension motivates abusive spouses to act in accord with the community's *do's* and *don'ts*.

Authorities' threats tend to have consequences that are opposite to those produced by the system's fair, just treatment of wrongdoers. Threats create boundaries between misbehaving spouses and the community. Consequently, *their*—the community's—rules do not become a guide to *my* behavior.

External threats might deter domestic abuse as the certainty of surveillance grows. But, as a practical matter, because surveillance over these events is typically uncertain, threats are documented to be a far less effective way of reducing domestic abuse than the ever-present internal constraint that results from feeling membership in a *we*-group with the forbidding rule, *Don't do it!*

The accumulated research evidence supports a straightforward claim: When employees are tied to their employers by bonds of *we*, *promotive tension* fuels the psychological golden rule of organizations. Subsequently, those employees are more likely to be motivated to work in ways that advance organization goals and restrain themselves from giving in to self-serving impulses that are likely to hinder organization goal achievement. This is the good news.

We Are Better

The bad news is that the very same psychological infrastructure makes it possible for *us* to work toward *their* destruction. It happens within organizations, when employees and bosses see each other across the barriers of *they*, and it happens between one organization and others, when members of that organization embrace each other as *we* while feeling separated by barriers of *they* from any other institutions in the community.

Once others are seen across a barrier of *they*, the mental ground is fertile for growing a socially destructive array of in-group, out-group distinctions. Stereotypes of *them* and *us* become increasingly different, as members of *we* tend to overestimate their similarity to one another and their dissimilarity from members of *they*. These exaggerations of similarity and difference grow even greater whenever the surrounding social atmosphere carries even the slightest whiff of competition between *them* and *us*. When barriers of *they* are present, faint hints of competition stimulate judgments that *we are better*. It is a foundation for mutual destruction. Blemishing *them* with the mark of Cain, while imagining *us* to be on God's side, paves the way for guilt-free efforts to benefit ourselves while harming *them*.

In organizations, this dark side of the bonds of *we* has at least two important consequences: It is a major contributor to a problem that is ravaging firms everywhere, *employee theft*, and it contributes to *we-boosting*, which are efforts to elevate *our* status by diminishing *theirs*.

Employee Theft

Thefts by employees impose an annual, multibillion-dollar tax on businesses. Some investigators claim that the problem is so severe that it is the cause of 30 percent to 50 percent of business failures.[6] Even if they are wrong by a factor of two, or as much as four, it still means that lots of businesses are suffering massive harm because of thefts by their employees.

Some explain the problem by blaming a few workers, whom they denounce as *bad apples*, claiming that the thieves are incorrigible carriers of character flaws. Others discount character, contending that low wages are causing employee theft. Workers, they say, are like hungry people who steal loaves of bread. They resort to theft in order to rectify real-life deprivations that are being caused by their inadequate incomes. These two explanations account for only a portion of the reasons why employees steal from their employers.

Workers who steal from employers often have high wages; they frequently steal things that cannot be transformed into assets that will improve their financial well being; and, most importantly, there is consistent evidence that employee theft is a product of social circumstances created by the employees' firms. After reviewing this evidence, one of the area's leading investigators concluded, "…good management, not necessarily more security equipment, is the route to lower levels of employee theft."[7]

Workers steal from employers who treat them disrespectfully and tend not to steal from those who treat them respectfully.[8] Barriers of *they*, erected by disrespectful employers, sever legal fact from psychological truth. Although statutes might legally define taking company property as unlawful, when barriers of *they* exist between employers and employees, workers who steal and coworkers who witness the theft tend not to see the deed as wrongdoing. In fact, stealing from *them*—the employer outgroup—occasionally is even regarded as a virtuous act, rather than a criminal one. Workers say, *It's not a big deal for* them; They *deserve what they get*; We *need and deserve the property more than* They *do*; and They *owe me.*

What to do? Help the psychological golden rule of organization to operate by observing five guidelines:

1. *Pay attention to the three Rs of organization life: Rewards, Respect, and Recognition.* Bonds of *we* include workers' employing

organizations when management of the three **R**s causes employees to utter a clear "Yes" to statements like the following: *Criticism of my organization feels like a personal insult. In talking about my organization, I say "we" rather than "they." My organization's successes are my successes.*[9] Stealing from *us* is a lot more difficult than stealing from *them.*

2. *Involve employees in defining theft.* Their involvement, as much as and probably more than the content of the definition that evolves, is a deterrent to subsequent employee theft. Every organizational effort to give employees genuine opportunities for voice accords them respect, producing bonds of *we* and buy-in.

3. *Communicate the costs of stealing.* In the case of employees who have mentally moved the organization icon to the *we* side of the *we/they* boundary, theft is more likely to be deterred if they understand the extent to which harm affects *us.*

4. *Create organization hotlines.* The content of what employees say, given the opportunity, might have practical benefit, and the process of providing them credible opportunities for voice will have relational benefit. It nudges the organization icon further into the *we* side of the *we/they* boundary.

5. *Model ethical behavior.* Dispense with special, elite privileges. Maintaining these privileges establishes a double standard, favoring employers over employees. In employees' minds, these different standards raise the barriers that divide *them* (employers) from *us* (employees), thereby lowering constraints against employee theft.

We-Boosting: Elevating *Our* Status by Diminishing *Theirs*

One of the most important experimental manifestations of *we*-boosting was first observed in the early 1970s in England, at the University of Bristol's psychology laboratories.[10] Since that first report, *we*-boosting has been recorded dozens of times, in the most ordinary settings as well as in research laboratories, by investigators working in Europe, the United States, and Australia.[11]

In the very first experiment of this decades-long series of investigations, 32 young men sat in groups of 8 watching 40 clusters of dots flash on a screen. After each cluster appeared and disappeared, the men had to guess the number of dots that it contained. With bogus scientific solemnity their guesses were recorded, analyzed, and reported back. Privately, four of the young men from each group of eight were told that they were part of a group of people who tend to *underestimate* the number of dots that clusters contain. Opposite, and equally false, information was privately supplied to the other four young men from each of the groups. They were told that they were part of a group of people who tend to *overestimate* the number of dots that clusters contain.

The fact that the group labels, *under-* and *over-estimator,* were trivial and totally contrived makes what happened next all the more interesting. After being told which group they were a part of because of their personal dot-judging tendency, the young men were separated and required to decide how an amount of money was to be distributed between two of the other young men—one of them was an *over-estimator* and the other was an *under-estimator.* Their decisions, which would forever remain secret, were not going to have any effect on how much money they themselves received.

People prefer to believe that if they were in the same situation, they would disregard the group labels and divide the money equally. Evidence from more than two decades of research with people of all ages, who grew up in different cultures and were given varying kinds of assets to distribute to similar and dissimilar others, proves that this self-serving belief is wrong. People in this experimental situation do what people working in organizations also do when they are separated from others across barriers of *they.* Resorting to *we*-boosting, they elevate *us* by diminishing *them.*

The young men from Bristol chose distributions that maximized the *difference* between what members of *we* and *they* received. Remarkably, they were so intent on maximizing differences between themselves and the others that they preferred options creating that distinction to other options that provided monetary differences between *under-estimators* and *over-estimators* that were smaller, but overall profits for members of *we* that were greater! Evidence from city streets, research laboratories, and organizations provides the same lesson: Looking at someone across barriers of *they* produces powerful motives to boost *we*, including *me*, by diminishing *them.*

Under the influence of these motives, bosses striving to raise their elite status find it personally satisfying to violate each of the three **R**s of organization life (**R**ewards, **R**espect, and **R**ecognition). Onlookers who lack any awareness of the pressure of these underlying motives might be puzzled by what they see as bosses' continuing greed, disrespect, and autocracy in the face of both common sense and a steady stream of empirical evidence showing that this managerial misconduct inflicts great harm on employees' productivity, commitment, and well-being. In order for observers to resolve the seeming paradox of this boss behavior, they must recognize that the behavior is not occurring merely because bosses crave the comfort of better cars, bigger houses, or more clothing.

Creature comforts count, of course. But if these comforts were the only reason, then bosses would be more responsive to the organizational harm that the message of their misbehavior causes, since that harm diminishes organizational returns that could be plundered by them for still more creature comfort.

Their aim, like that of the young men from Bristol, is to increase the *difference* in outcomes to *them* and *us*, not just to increase the outcomes to *us*. In addition to providing creature comfort, bosses' greedy, disrespectful, autocratic behaviors are recognized symbols of their status. These behaviors boost the bosses' status because they are messages about how elite *we* are in comparison to other members of the workforce. Sadly, for too many bosses, their favored ways of boosting *we*, including *me*, require diminishing *thee*.

Every time that bosses grant themselves special rewards, show that they are free to do unto subordinates what subordinates are not free to do unto them, and stifle employees' voices by autocratically exercising their power, they send the workforce messages that erode bonds of *we* and erect barriers of *they*. Although these *we*-boosting behaviors harm organizations and their constituencies, they continue because they permit a rewarding elevation in the image that bosses have about their own status.

Because of bosses' arrogant *we*-boosting behavior, when members of the workforce ask themselves the critical question about the three **R**s of organization life (*Am I treated fairly, with civility, and proper recognition of my abilities?*), the answer they give is "No." Employees' productivity, commitment, and well-being subsequently suffer.

Organizations and their constituencies lose. But none of this deters the bosses who cause these costs. They might not like the losses, but they appear to love the status gains produced by *we*-boosting. Something must be done.

[1] McKinley, J. C. Jr. "It isn't just a game: Clues to avid rooting." *New York Times* (August 11, 2000): A1, D5.

[2] Hornstein, H. A. *Cruelty and Kindness: A New Look at Aggression and Altruism* (New Jersey: Prentice Hall, 1976).; Hornstein, H. A. "Promotive tension: The basis of prosocial behavior from a Lewinian perspective." *Journal of Social Issues* 28 (1976): 191–218.; Hornstein, H. A. "Promotive tension theory and research." In V. S. Derlega and J. Grzelak (Eds.) *Cooperation and Helping Behavior: Theory and Research* (New York: Academic Press, 1982): 229–248.

[3] Hornstein, H. A., H. N. Masor, K. Sole, and M. Heilman. "Effects of sentiment and completion of a helping act on observer helping: A case for socially mediated Zeigarnik effects." *Journal of Personality and Social Psychology* 17 (1971): 107–112.; Hodgson, S. A., H. A. Hornstein, and E. LaKind. "Socially mediated Zeigarnik effects as a function of sentiment, valance, and desire for goal attainment." *Journal of Experimental Social Psychology* 8 (1972): 446–456.

[4] Tyler, T. R. and P. Degoey. "Trust in organizational authorities." In T. R. Tyler and R. M. Kramer (Eds.) *Trust in Organizations: Frontiers of Theory and Research* (Thousand Oaks, CA: Sage, 1996): 331–356.

[5] "Misconceptions about why people obey laws and accept judicial decisions." *APS Observer* (September, 1997).

[6] Greenberg, J., and K. S. Scott. "Why do workers bite the hands that feed them? Employee theft as a social exchange process." *Research in Organizational Behavior* 18 (1996): 111–156.

[7] Hollinger, R. C. *Dishonesty in the Workplace: A Manager's Guide to Preventing Employee Theft.* (Park Ridge, Ill.: London House, 1989): 35.

[8] Altheide, D. L., P. A. Adler, P. Adler, and D. A. Altheide. "The social meanings of employee theft." In J. M. Johnson and J. D. Douglas (Eds.) *Crime at the Top: Deviance in Business and the Professions* (Philadelphia, PA: J.B. Lippencott, 1978): 90–124.

[9] A complete presentation of these statements are presented in this book's first chapter. They are adapted from F. A. Mael and B. E. Ashforth. "Identifying organization identification." *Educational And Psychological Measurement* 52 (1995): 813–824.

[10] Tajfel, H., C. Flament, M. G. Billig, and R. F. Bundy. "Social categorization and intergroup behavior." *European Journal of Social Psychology* 1 (1971): 149–177.

[11] Tajfel, H. (Ed.). *Differentiation between Social Groups: Studies in the Social Psychology of Intergroup Relations* (London: Academic Press, 1978); Turner, J. C., M. A. Hogg, P. J. Oakes, S. D. Reicher, and M. S. Wetherell. (Eds.). *Rediscovering the Social Group: A Self-Categorization Theory* (Oxford, England: Basil Blackwell, 1987); Ellemers, N., R. Spears, and B. Doosje. (Eds.). *Social Identity: Context, Commitment, Content* (Oxford, England: Basil Blackwell, 1999).

7

AFFIRMING EMPLOYEES: TO *US* FROM *THEM*

Use whatever words you choose—*ambition, ego, showing-off*, or *status seeking*—the fact is that bosses' *we*-boosting is the result of human inclinations from which no one is totally immune and, in organizations, boss misbehavior stemming from *we*-boosting is capable of derailing success. That is the bad news. The good news is that organizations can stop enabling these misbehaviors. Something can be done.

"Work-Out," a concept so valuable that GE has trademarked the term itself, illustrates one solution. "Work-Outs, begun in 1989, are meetings that can be called by anybody to address any problem ... with no boss in the room." Once a plan to solve the problem has been developed, bosses are obliged to respond with an unambiguous *yes* or *no*. "Work-Outs have become so common that there's probably one every day in each sizable GE facility, without management's knowing about it till someone pops in saying 'We had a Work-Out and need to talk to you.'" A GE employee described the resulting culture as one in which, *"Teamwork is key, not authority."* In his words, *"All the best ideas come from teams."*[1]

The genius of Work-Out, (as well as QMI—the acronym for "Quick Meeting Intelligence"—a WalMart diagnostic meeting procedure also used by GE), is that it clearly says to the entire workforce, *Solving work problems is not the special preserve of a powerful privileged elite called "The Bosses."* In fact, the procedure's implicit message is that sometimes bosses so lack what is needed for problem solving, listening is the best way for them to lead.

The Container Store, the first-ranked company on *Fortune*'s January 10, 2000 list of the best 100 companies to work for, and second-ranked in its 2001 listing, also implements policies that are an antidote to the human inclination toward *we*-boosting: "... The Container Store promises only that it will treat its workers like humans. Grade-school-type maxims—treat people as you want to be treated, help others—are granted policy status. And instead of tightly guarding financial information, The Container Store opens its ledger to all employees. The outcomes ...losing just 28 percent of its full-time sales people a year, vs. the industry average of 73.6 percent, and just 5.3 percent of its store managers, compared with the industry's 33.6 percent."[2]

The Container Store's practices limit bosses' *we*-boosting wriggle room by defining every member of a firm's workforce as part of *we*. They announce loudly and clearly that when the firm granted some of its members temporary power over others, it was not also giving them license to create disaffirming, self-serving rules of conduct.

The Container Store's anti-*we*-boosting practices, along with those like GE's Work-Out, contradict Frederick Taylor's employee disaffirming advice that "all possible brain work should be removed from the shop."[3] In fact, the opposite is true: Organizations are only able to inhibit bosses' *we*-boosting inclinations when they introduce unambiguously consistent policies and procedures that express their commitment to affirming the whole employee—*as a contributor to the firm's operations; as a worker who is part of the community's job market; as a member of groups outside the firm that make legitimate demands (families, religious institutions, and civic associations); and as an individual with physical and psychological needs.*

Affirm Employees as Contributors

Jacques Nasser joined Ford Australia in 1968 as a financial analyst. Before that, he had managed a bicycle-making business and a discotheque. Thirty years later, he was Ford Motor Company's Chief Executive Officer.

During his time as Ford's CEO, Mr. Nasser made it an acknowledged goal to transform the company into a united enterprise in which employees think and act like owners, from one in which the firm's operating divisions were managed as if they were senior managers' fiefdoms. Regardless of alleged shortcomings that contributed to his departure from Ford in 2001, for pursuing this goal he deserves praise. His business case for creating a united enterprise is straightforward: "*The capital markets are ruthless. They don't care about the stellar performance of our design team, or the financial results of a particular geographic region, or the amazing productivity of one molding plant. The capital markets value the health of a company as a whole. Is the company positioned to meet its customers' needs while bringing home greater returns on the capital employed?*"[4]

Continuing his emphasis on the business need to think of *us*, one company, and not *I*, Mr. Nasser added, "The markets reward the kinds of companies in which, for instance, a manager at an assembly plant in Cologne says, 'It would definitely lower my costs to change such-and-such a supplier, but it would change our global strategy for raw material sourcing. I won't do it.... What can I do to make this whole company work better and smarter and faster? What creative ideas do I have that will really make us grow, not just in my case, but over there, in that division or that one?'"[5]

Guided by CEO Nasser's pursuit of this goal, bosses at each level must cooperate with their direct reports in order to discover how the unit might better contribute to the organization's change goals and initiatives. These programs, which affected 55,000 salaried workers, employed 360-degree feedback, community service, and a 100-day project during which employees develop usable plans for cost savings or new revenue sources. Nasser estimated that these programs produced a $2 billion bottom-line benefit for Ford. For example, one group worked on a project aimed at doubling the productivity and halving the time of IT (information technology) systems development. The projected savings was $40 million.

One peg supporting Ford's change strategy was University of Michigan Professor Noel Tichy's concept of the *teachable point of view*.[6] Applications of this concept to organizations require bosses to become teachers of their subordinates who, in turn, teach their subordinates. In Tichy's words, a teachable point of view *is about what a person knows and believes about what it takes to succeed in his or her business as well as in business generally*.[7]

The process is not for the faint-hearted or the arrogant. It results in an exposure of bosses' beliefs about consumers, competition, market forces, and technology, as well as the firm's future business contours and their implications for personnel policy, structure, and strategy. The process also affirms employees as contributors, transforming *I* into *we*. Beginning at the top of the organization, bosses start meetings with their subordinates by describing the four principle components of their *teachable point of view*:

> **Ideas**—What are your beliefs about current and future characteristics of consumers, competition, market forces, and technology, and their implications for personnel policy, structure, and strategy?
>
> **Values**—What are your guiding principles?
>
> **Emotional energy**—How do you motivate employees?
>
> **Edge**—When and how do you go about making tough decisions?

Working together, leaders and subordinates then discuss, debate, and, if necessary, reformulate these teachable points of view.[8]

Tichy reports that Jacques Nasser and his senior group inaugurated the process at Ford by going through this experience at four off-site meetings over a four-month period. Afterward, this group's boss/teachers shared, debated, and reformulated their own views with their subordinates, who then conducted similar meetings with their subordinates, and so on, until the process cascaded through the entire organization.

Surely there are immediate tangible benefits to making all employees' teachable points of view explicit. The information sharing smoothes intra-individual consistency, meshes inter-individual expectations, and enhances coordination within and between work units. But procedures like Tichy's also have longer-term, less tangible organization benefits. Genuine conversation creates bonds. Concealment is divisive. Properly managed face-to-face discussion produces exposure and vulnerability for all participants, regardless of rank. It erodes elitism and broadens the boundaries of *we*.

One-way lectures of the very same content assisted by dull slide shows build barriers of *they*, allowing boss elites to preach from on high. Podiums become obstructions to protect existing practices, silencing employees' voices by defining *them* as noncontributors.

When employees are genuinely free to ask their boss/teachers for greater clarity, safely offer modifications to what has been said, or voice dissent, tangible improvement of bosses' ideas can result, as well as an affirmation of all employees' roles as valued contributors. To understand why organizational procedures like Tichy's have these effects requires that we recognize the difference between *Final Authority* and *Complete Authority*:

Final Authority *is a matter of hierarchical position. It identifies who in the organization possesses the legitimate power to either authorize or veto action.*

Complete Authority *is a matter of competence. It identifies who in the organization possesses knowledge that might contribute to solving a particular work problem.*

Organizations cannot function effectively without clearly defining *Final Authority.* Hierarchy, which is simply the stacking of positions according to *Final Authority*, does not cause *we*-boosting problems if the prescribed authorities are nonoverlapping and suited to task requirements. *We*-boosting problems arise in organizations when policy and procedure permit bosses to act as if they had *Complete Authority*, when they don't. Those isolated and isolating "I-know–it-all" actions send messages of exclusion that disaffirm employees as contributors, erect boss/elites, and nullify the psychological golden rule of organizations: *Harming you becomes difficult for me because the two of us are part of* we.

A new tool for organization problem solving, *whole system intervention* is also a powerful means of affirming employees as contributors precisely because it does not allow a small band of bosses to act as if they had *Complete Authority*.[9] Ford has used *whole system* organizational problem-solving procedures to facilitate the opening of a new plant. U.S. West has used them to set strategic priorities. And Boeing has used them to help in the development of its 777 jetliners.[10]

Whole system interventions are designed to improve many familiar organizational processes such as product development, responses to legal regulations, financing strategy, technical progress, and personnel policy. What distinguishes these interventions from more traditional organizational efforts to discuss the same issues is who gets involved in the discussions.

Instead of having a small, 8 or 10-person task force secreted in some organizational cranny concocting solutions, *whole system interventions* have scores of employees, from various levels and functions, as well as customers and even vendors, working on analysis and action planning. In this way, problem solutions affirm employees as contributors (and customers and vendors, too), while unequivocally declaring that problem solving is not the province of elite bosses who use their position as a basis for claiming *Complete Authority*.

Whole system interventions come in different packages, each with its own nuance. For example, *Future Search Conferences* employ structured agendas and exercises, *Open Space Meetings* work without any preset agenda, and *The Conference Model*, a procedure often used as an aid in organization redesign, employs four, well-spaced, structured, two- or three-day meetings. The common element transcending the approaches' different nuances is that everyone who is affected by the work or its outcome participates, sometimes causing the attendance to reach jaw-dropping levels.

In 1993, for example, Ford brought 2,400 employees together to plan the opening of a Mustang plant. And, when Boeing worked on developing the 777, meetings conducted under CEO Phil Condit's guidance included as many as 5,000 people. Using some extraordinary logistical expertise that solicits and uses individual input despite group size, these procedures increase the opportunity for having the right information and ideas at the right place at the right time. They also make the transfer of agreed-upon actions back into the workplace easier because personnel involved in making the transition were also involved in preparing what needs to be transferred. But, more than anything else, *whole system intervention* problem-solving procedures build connecting bonds of *we* by affirming the value of employees as contributors.

Mergers are also times that afford businesses opportunities to affirm or disaffirm their employees as contributors. The problem faced by merging firms is how to make *we* out of *them* and *us*? The sad statistics of mergers tell us that the correct solution to this problem is often missed. Perhaps as many as 75 percent of mergers fail to achieve their promises in cost-savings, increased market share, technological synergies, or customer access.[11]

Bob Bauman, Beecham's CEO at the time that firm merged with Smith-Kline Beckman, explained, "...it was important to change the focus from being, 'Here are two old companies. We're going to bring them together and take the best of each' to 'We're going to create a totally new company that's able to compete in the future.'"[12]

In order to achieve this shift of focus, the heads of regional units in the two firms joined their staffs in working to identify and align values, leadership behaviors, and performance measures for the new organization. From a practical perspective, this format created performance measures that had the best possible chance of driving leadership behaviors that were deliberately designed to be consistent with expressed values. From an organization perspective, the widespread involvement of different-level personnel from the two organizations both affirmed employees as contributors and discredited the idea that an isolated group of elite bosses could successfully mandate the future organization's design.

Moving into the age of e-business afforded Jack Welch, GE's former CEO, with the opportunity to introduce anti-*we*-boosting policies that affirmed GE's employees as contributors. With his customary perspicacity, Mr. Welch described the sea of change that the Web's arrival was causing GE: *"It will change relationships with employees. We will never again have discussions where knowledge is hidden in somebody's pocket. You will have to lead with ideas, not by controlling information.... It will change relationships with customers. Customers will see everything. Nothing will be hidden in paperwork.... It will change relationships with suppliers. Within 18 months, all our suppliers will supply us on the Internet or they won't do business with us."*[13]

As part of his effort to thrust GE in the e-business direction, Jack Welch empowered mavericks, people who are free to break company rules (albeit, without violating company values). Every GE business was urged to have one, and rank was not identified as a criterion for the maverick's selection. Instead, these maverick-employees, who reported directly to a business' CEO, had to be e-business buffs. Their job was to mature GE as an e-business by flushing out the old and installing the new.

Mr. Welch also decided that GE's modernization would be helped if his top managers (about 600 of them) learned how to surf the Web. The message: *Reach down and find someone in your organization that can be your mentor.* Practicing what he preached, CEO Jack Welch reached down to Ms. Pat Wickham, a 37-year-old who ran GE's Web site. Certainly, if GE's 600 top managers followed their CEO's example, then there was a good chance that they would learn how to surf the Web. But Mr. Welch's words and actions were not just about moving his firm into the e-business age. There was a subtext that communicated a message about the organization. Through its use of mavericks and mentors, GE was affirming its employees' as contributors, because of their proficiencies, regardless of rank.

Affirm Employees as Workers

By the time Corey Thomas graduated from Nashville, Tennessee's Vanderbilt University in 1998, he already had a point-of-view about how he should handle employers' regard for their employees: *My dad worked for Sears for 19 years as a security guard, and then he was laid off. I have to position myself so I can constantly watch out for myself. I have to be self-serving.*[14]

A man who was fired from his job and then re-employed as a Connecticut tourist guide, taking a month to earn what he once earned in a week, arrived at the same conclusion: *"My state of mind now is looking out for No. 1."*[15]

Freshman and veteran members of the workforce, like Corey Thomas and the man who was re-employed as a Connecticut tourist guide, are not fools. Working people are naturally drawn to the conclusion that self-serving behavior is essential when employers make it evident that their orientation toward workers is instrumental, spelled out in the renowned *we*-boosting slogan, *What did* you *do for* us *today?*

An instrumental organizational orientation toward employees has its defenders. Some businesspeople, economists, and behavioral scientists argue that in today's competitive world, organizations' survival would be threatened if bosses were not instrumental in their dealings with employees. They are wrong. Protecting a firm's competitive edge might require decisions that are disapproved by employees, but being instrumental is always bad for business.

Businessman Michael Price reportedly owned 21 percent of Sunbeam when Albert Dunlap was hired as the company's CEO. When Mr. Dunlap decided to fire 6,000 Sunbeam employees, Mr. Price sounded pleased. "Those jobs were gone anyway," he was quoted as saying. "It's part of our economy. Look at France. They protect jobs there, and the whole economy suffers."[16] Regardless of whether Mr. Price is correct in assuming that the whole French economy suffers because of France's job protection measures, the rest of his logic is faulty. He was speaking as if firms are limited to just two options: dismissal or guaranteed employment.

Some economists contend that the first of these options, dismissal, is clearly superior. They argue that the pruning of organizations' payrolls benefits workers by lowering production costs, producing ripple effects that ultimately create new jobs elsewhere in the economy. "You can't make a prosperity omelet without breaking eggs," explained one writer, colorfully summarizing the viewpoint of these economists.[17] While another reveals to us that "Corporations were put on this earth, after all, to make money, and to some minds, profit maximization will never seem all that different from greed. But profits, of course, pay for the latest equipment and technology that produce economic growth and more jobs. If corporations weren't greedy like that, they'd go out of business, and then we'd all be in trouble."[18]

The Connecticut tourist guide, for example, who was a victim of one organization's downsizing, might have been subsequently re-employed by another organization precisely because the first organization's improved profits, stemming from lower labor costs, prompted increased demand that eventually led other organizations to hire additional employees. So, these defenders wonder, why is there all this whining about downsizing when it is doing so much economic good? What they fail to understand is that the macro-economic benefits for society that might be attributable to downsizing are too remote to relieve the immediate worries of workers who are threatened with a job loss.

These workers are worried about tomorrow's housing payments, and about their upcoming bills for medical care, groceries, insurance, auto repair, and school tuition. When downsizing efforts, shaped by calloused, matter-of-fact, instrumental orientations neglect these concerns, they cause workers to feel alienated from both their instrumentally oriented bosses and the business community that these bosses represent. "I have to be self-serving," says it all. Clearly, if downsizing is the required remedy for what ails an organization, then the downsizing should not be managed by bosses who hold instrumental orientations if the organization wants to avoid the adverse effects of employee alienation.

Instrumentally oriented bosses' decision making is not greatly affected by workers' worries. Their primary guide is the achievement of immediate, measurable cost savings while cautiously adhering to the letter of any applicable legal constraints. For them to do either more or less than whatever those constraints require adds avoidable costs, and that is a violation of their prime guideline: achieve financial cost savings. Without apology, the message that these bosses send to employees is:

After you have been dismissed from this organization, your *vocational afterlife is not* our *concern.*

Support for this disaffirmation of employees as workers also comes from the slant that some behavioral scientists have given to the new employment contract. By arguing that employee loyalty nowadays is to work (to one's profession or skill), not to employers, they have left the impression that instrumentality is in. It's okay to be expedient and self-serving. Everyone's doing it. It's expected.

This argument creates two problems: First, it overlooks an obvious question:

If employees' loyalties are not to their employing firms, might it be because bitter experience has taught them not to expect employers to give them the Rewards, Respect, and Recognition that they deserve?

Second, by putting this slant on their interpretation of the new employment contract, behavioral scientists take the monkey off managers' backs. Instrumentally oriented bosses are handed an expert justification for having no concern at all with employees' futures as workers. The resulting behaviors are harsh, moving the organization icon just a little deeper into *they* territory.

This criticism of those businesspeople, economists, and behavioral scientists that defend instrumental organization orientations is *not* an argument for ruling out dismissals as organizational option. Certainly, organizations are not obliged to commit financial suicide by guaranteeing employment. But, instead of the new employment contract's instrumental you're-on-your-own approach, remedies are needed that communicate that every employee's tomorrow is on this organization's list of today's responsibilities.

Those are the only remedies that have a chance of triggering the psychological golden rule of organizations, causing employees to incorporate the organization's tomorrow into their own list of today's responsibilities. Thus, maintaining an alternative to the two extremes of dismissal and guaranteed employment requires affirming employees as workers who have vocational concerns that go beyond their immediate employment. One way to communicate that affirmation is to commit an organization to efforts that result in employees' enhanced employability.

Jobs that add to workers' repertoire of skills or vocational reputation naturally enhance employability. Workers benefiting from this enhancement have the luxury of facing a beckoning job market optimistically, knowing that their resumes were strengthened by their previous employment. Unfortunately, jobs can also have the opposite consequence. They can diminish and even extinguish future employability if, while doing the particular work required by an employer, workers must step off the career ladder, losing opportunity for any meaningful vocational development. When work threatens employees with these losses, workers, their employers, and the entire business community benefit if firms make deliberate efforts to enhance their workforces' future employability.

One example of such an effort was an AT&T project called Resource Link.[19] In this case, an "internal contingent workforce" staffed by displaced managers and professionals was assigned temporarily (for three months to a year) to projects across the company. Reports indicate that the effort provided AT&T with greater staffing flexibility and employees with both stability and development.

A variation on this internal workforce theme, a redeployment procedure used by Intel, is another example of an effort at enhancing employability. This procedure once helped the firm avert mass layoffs by successfully relocating between 80 percent and 90 percent of Intel employees who needed to find new jobs because their old ones disappeared. Intel employee development centers supported redeployment by providing workers with opportunities for assessment, guidance, training, and Intel job listings. If all these opportunities failed to produce an internal placement, then outplacement assistance was also available.[20]

Other companies affirm employees as workers by providing them with college support, funded apprenticeships, and vouchers to use for retraining. Trustmark Insurance, for example, a Lake Forest, Illinois company, recruited employees who volunteered to be trained as computer programmers. Trustmark then not only paid for the employees' college-level classes, but also provided them with mentors to help with material being presented in the classes. BGS Systems Inc., in Waltham, Massachusetts, and Hewlett-Packard, also have provided courses for software engineers who want to upgrade their skills.[21] All this is low-hanging fruit. It is nothing new, but it is also not a particularly common practice either. That is shameful.

In 1997, several companies (AT&T, Dupont, GTE, Johnson & Johnson, Lucent, TRW Unisys, and UPS) joined Talent Alliance, a system on the Web that provides employees with opportunities for vocational assessment, information regarding training at company expense, and job postings in the member companies.[22] Through their involvement in Talent Alliance, these companies were sending a message: *We accept our responsibility to work with employees in order to help them enhance their employability.*

Efforts like Talent Alliance represent responsible affirmation of employees as workers, not patronizing welfare. Nothing is being given away. Nor are these efforts organizationally self-defeating guarantees of employment. By accepting a partner's responsibility for enhancing employees' future employability, these adjuncts to cost-cutting remedies send an anti-*we*-boosting message to bosses, employees, and the political communities that guard employees' health and welfare. The message says that although tough decisions might have to be made, instrumentalism is out. Employees, who are part of we, are not commodities to be used and then abruptly discarded according to our immediate needs.

Affirm Employees as Members of Outside Groups

What happens when employees bring work issues into their homes is only half the subject matter that should be of concern to work-family experts.

The rest of their concern should be with what happens in organizations when employees bring issues from home into the workplace.

Children's booster seats and highchairs have been familiar additions to the cafeteria's decor at Freddie Mac, the McLean, Virginia mortgage firm. "Employees applaud the highchairs as an effective work-and-family benefit. Even workers without young children welcome the junior visitors," said one observer. And, an employee, whose two-year old was one of those occasional visitors reported, "It makes people smile." [23]

People smile because this type of organization outreach pleases them. Perhaps that is why there is surprisingly broad agreement about how beneficial it might be to organizations if their policies helped employees to manage obligations that they cannot possibly leave behind at the factory gates. A poll of 300 companies reported by the Chicago-based Canon Consulting Group showed that 72 percent of the firms believed that absenteeism would be reduced if companies provided onsite or off-site support for children's day-care services. The sad fact is that in 1996, when the poll was conducted, only 6 percent of the 300, a mere 18 companies, followed their own wisdom by providing their employees with help for day-care services.[24] The availability of these services improved only slightly six years later, in 2002, when Hewitt Associates reported that the number of U.S. companies providing onsite day care had grown to 12 percent.[25]

Instead of providing full-time day-care services, Hewitt Associates reports that about 15 percent of companies provide employees with access to backup care in the event their regular arrangements are disrupted by emergencies such as their children's or babysitter's illness.[26] There is payoff for providing this backup perk according to 90 percent of the employees surveyed at J.P. Morgan Chase, who say that their availability boosted employee morale and productivity. And payoff is also registered on the bottom line according to data from Goldman Sachs. They report that in 2001, the value of workdays saved because of backup care was $1.3 million, nearly double their cost of maintaining the program.[27]

From a realm at the other end of the chronological spectrum, elder care, comes some mildly encouraging evidence that organizations have been increasingly willing to undertake programs that help employees deal with their outside (that is, non-work-generated) obligations. Because of increasing life spans, elder care is an issue of growing importance.

At the turn of the millennium, more than 21 million U.S. families were helping aging relatives. "Elder care is driving a growing number of job changes. That's a shift from the past, when these caregivers were typically older women who eventually quit work. Now, the average caregiver is more likely to be an executive, manager, or professional, or a family breadwinner of any stripe, who is unable or unwilling to drop out."[28]

Typically, companies help employees deal with their obligations to care for aging relatives in three ways—by offering resource and referral programs, dependent care spending accounts, or long-term care insurance. Forty-seven percent of the companies questioned in a 1999 Hewitt Associates survey reported that they provided one or more of these three forms of support. That was up from 20 percent just a few years earlier, in 1993.[29]

Let's applaud the programs' growth among firms, but also ask, "How many *employees* in these companies are actually eligible to receive these benefits?" If eligibility is limited, then there is a danger that the programs might have a boomerang effect, increasing in the gap between the eligible, elite we, and the ineligible remainder of the workforce, who protest, "Why not us also?"

Work-family life programs that help employees to meet their child and elder care obligations advance organizational progress toward two desired outcomes: First, by lifting practical burdens from employees' shoulders they ease their minds and remove workplace distractions. Second, these programs help organizations progress toward the goal of inhibiting bosses' *we*-boosting by announcing to the entire workforce that, *This company's concern is with you as a person, whose membership in groups outside the organization creates obligations that affect your work. Its concern is not just with you as a worker, who must be helped to fulfill only those obligations that arise because of the work task that you were assigned.*

Events that began in a small clothing store in an Ohio shopping center show how senior management's regard for these obligations can boost business success while becoming a powerful antidote to *we*-boosting. In only two decades, that store grew into the Limited, Inc., a firm that included Express, Structure, Victoria's Secret, and Abercrombie & Fitch. But fortunes change, and 10 years later, in 1993, with Limited's growth stalling badly, its founder, Leslie Wexner, worked to restore its success by reconfiguring the organization's policies, procedures, and his own approach to management.[30] His efforts were rewarded: Limited's growth resumed and its stock traded at peak values.

Leslie Wexner explained his success: In the reconfigured organization "the nine retail brands are encouraged to work together, sharing information and holding monthly meetings of divisional heads who had been fierce sibling-rivals under the old structure." In addition, he confessed that his managerial style shifted to one that is broadly concerned about the workplace from one that was more narrowly concerned only about work: "When I talked with Calloway (that's Wayne Calloway, former CEO of Pepsico, Inc.), I asked how he spent his time. And he said that he probably spent ... 40 percent or 50 percent of his time on people. To me it was startling. I like people, but I'm busy picking sweaters, visiting stores, doing things. How do you find that much time?"

Leslie Wexner found the time. Now, when he considers people for positions, he looks for three things: First, do they know their jobs? Second, are they whole people? Do they have balanced lives? Do they care about community? And the third attribute that he assesses in selecting among job candidates is a person's "true sense of responsibility for the people that they are working with. That they not only say it, but they demonstrate that they really care about the people that they work with. You can't fake that."

If these selection criteria are actually employed, and if they are one part of a company's consistent effort to affirm the whole employee, then they are capable of nourishing the growth of an anti-*we*-boosting culture by putting bosses on notice that they are not free to disregard the outside obligations that employees bring into the workplace.

Affirm Employees as Individuals with Physical and Psychological Needs

Scientific evidence proves conclusively that a work area's aromas, temperature, noise levels, and air quality affect employees' feelings and behaviors.[31] When these environmental conditions are agreeable, conflicts are less frequent and positive performance appraisals are more frequent.

But simple bodily sensations are not the sole reason that desirable work outcomes arise from favorable environmental conditions. Employees know that the environmental improvements are the product of organization decision-making. It is easy to understand that employees decipher one message when they believe that their employing organization cares enough about their physical well being to provide them with pleasant aromas and sound levels, but an entirely different message when they believe that *they* (their employers) don't care if *we* work amidst noxious smells and sounds.

Deliberate efforts to improve employees' physical well being broaden the boundaries of *we*. They say, *We're in this together. If it's not good for any one of us, then it's not good for any of us.* These efforts are anti-*we*-boosting messages. By contrast, organizations' deliberate disregard of their workforces' physical experiences narrow the boundaries of *we*. They invite *we*-boosting by tacitly telling bosses that it is OK to forget about *them*!

Organizational attention to employees' psychological needs can have the same anti-*we*-boosting effects as attention to their physical needs.

Taking a day to replenish personal batteries after completing a grueling patch of work can benefit employees' mental health with return benefits to employers. Experts believe that it is so, arguing that providing employees with well-being days can be as critical to maintaining their good health as ordinary sick days. But it is not a benefit that organizations commonly provide. Even when they do, as Catherine Heany, an Ohio State University researcher discovered, employees are often reluctant to avail themselves of the opportunity because they believe that their organization's culture is subtly unsupportive.[32]

Levi Strauss & Company can be applauded for a program that both provided the benefit and supported its use. Called TOPP (Time Off with Pay Program), the program encouraged employees to take time off for personal reasons when it was warranted. Jeff Friant, a Levi Strauss manager for staffing, explained why the time-off program succeeded in this company while it so frequently failed in others: "People who thoughtfully utilize TOPP time are seen as working for balance in their professional and personal lives. *People are admired for that.*" [33]

Web Industries, a Massachusetts-based manufacturing company, is another example of a company that uses time off as a means of attending to its workers' psychological needs. Web gives its workers time away from the job in order to read "thought provoking" books.[34]

Of course, free time is only one way for firms to show their concern for employees' psychological needs. Silicon Graphics Inc. of Mountain View, California, for example, does it by encouraging its employees to tap their creative juices. The firm awards the ones who write poems that best capture the company's ideals with vacation trips and a one-year membership in a management advisory group. And Marjorie Miller, who owns Miller & Associates, a wholesaler of kitchenware based in Dallas, Texas, has her employees include in their annual goals a self-analysis of satisfying experiences that they want to pursue in the future.[35]

Another alternative means of showing concern for employees' psychological needs comes from the efforts of approximately 4,000 ministers of all faiths who work in U.S. companies. Their loyalty is to their mission of helping employees, not to management. Reverend C. Alan Tyson, for example, worked at a chicken processing plant employing 1,600 people. He dealt with their troubles—drinking, drugs, marital conflict, illness, delinquent children, overdue mortgages, layoffs, and financial security.

One of the employees with whom Reverend Tyson worked was Fred Cantor, a processing line superintendent. Mr. Cantor needed help in dealing with a family member's drug problem. After working with Reverend Tyson, Mr. Cantor shared his feelings. "He helped me realize I wasn't alone."[36]

Ministering provides organizations with immediate practical benefit. It eases employees' problems. The caring conversation provides them with new perspectives for managing old concerns. They know that they are not alone. Each day, less stressed, less distracted workers arrive better prepared to do their jobs. By providing employees with any demonstration of caring—counselors of any type, time off for personal reasons, or opportunities for creative expression and self-reflection—companies also benefit by sending their entire workforce an anti-*we*-boosting message. *No elites here*, is what it says. *No members of this organization are free to treat any other members as if their needs are not our concern.*

Paternalism: Making *Them* into *Our* Burden

Worry about paternalism is an often-used reason for continuing conditions hospitable to bosses' *we*-boosting. But affirming employees as contributors to the firm's operations, as workers who are part of the community's job market, as members of groups outside of the firm that make legitimate demands (e.g., families, religious institutions, and civic associations), and as individuals with physical and psychological needs has nothing at all to do with paternalism.

Paternalism is care taking, doing *for* employees. Affirmation is doing *with* employees. As the examples given here show, affirming efforts provide members of the workforce with the room and resources they need in order to exercise their capabilities (affirming employees as contributors), develop vocational potential (affirming employees as workers), fulfill obligations (affirming employees as members of outside groups), and express needs (affirming employees as individuals with physical and psychological needs). Affirmation of the whole employee is an antidote to bosses' *we*-boosting precisely because it disavows paternalism. It says,

In this organization, no one is inferior. Therefore, there is no elite we *who must take care of* them, *and there is no less valued* they *who some anointed* we *is permitted to disregard.*

Modern versions of company towns can never be antidotes to bosses' *we*-boosting. On the contrary, regardless of bosses' honestly benevolent intentions, organizations that give things and build employees' dependency are doing today exactly what they did yesterday: Supporting the growth of a *we*-boosting elite who gives *them* handouts.

Paternalism is always a message of exclusion. In paternalistic organizations, bosses unilaterally decide the what, when, how, who, and where of their giving. Subordinates in these organizations are reduced to exchanging their obedience for their bosses' largess. Paternalism perverts the psychological golden rule of organizations from *Harming you becomes difficult for me because the two of us are part of we*, to *Harming you becomes difficult for me because of what my costs would be.* The result is employee conformity, not commitment. *They* are not truly a part of *us*.

What *We* Guarantees

By setting down consistent policies and procedures that affirm the whole employee, organizations can inhibit bosses' natural *we*-boosting tendencies while guiding them toward proper management of the three **R**s of organization life (**R**ewards, **R**espect, and **R**ecognition). Critics might object to this claim, saying that companies often succeed regardless of how well or how poorly their workforces are treated.

It's true: The healthy profits that a strong economy produces often overcome the adverse financial effects of internal organizational disease. Special, well-protected marketplace niches, a company's unique competencies, technological advances, and product innovations are similarly capable of producing profits for internally troubled organizations. But excellence is not forever. Competitors are on the prowl. Imitation and invention are steadily shortening the half-life of any business advantage.

No one can promise firms that building employees' organizational identity guarantees their financial success. All other things equal, however, those that do successfully build it can safely expect to extend their survival with the competitive edge of committed employees guided by the psychological golden rule of organizations.

An even stronger guarantee can be made to organizations whose bosses are freed to continue *we*-boosting. There is no guesswork here. Current events prove that these companies might just as well hang a sign over their entryways reading

> WE INVITE ALIENATED WORKERS,
> NEGATIVE PUBLIC OPINION,
> AND POLITICAL INTERVENTION

because that is precisely what they are going to get.

Today's news headlines promise that employees who continue to be the victims of *we*-boosting bosses will eventually seek help from third parties in order to offset their bosses' abuse of power. The tip of a very large government regulation iceberg is already above the surface.

Recently, the United States Bureau of Labor Statistics estimated that the country had approximately 3,000,000 "contingent workers." The count included "people who've worked on a job for a year or less and who expect to work there another year or less." Just 9.4 percent of this group had employee-sponsored health insurance, and only 13 percent were given opportunities for pension coverage.[37]

Displeased with this treatment of contingent workers, the AFL-CIO has been campaigning for laws that will prevent companies from classifying employees in this category. Because members of the category are denied the same legal protections as full-time colleagues, any restriction in the use of contingent workers would limit companies' freedom to offer diminished benefits.

Labor unions are not the only group in society concerned about companies' treatment of contingent workers. Since women typically have been disproportionately represented in this disadvantaged group, the AFL-CIO's lobbying efforts are being augmented by 9to5 (National Association of Working Women), whose co-director Ellen Bravo, contended, "From day laborers to higher-paid 'perma-temps,' ...these arrangements (i.e., contingent workers accepting lesser benefits) are neither voluntary nor equitable."[38] Seeking third-party help for their constituencies, these two groups, the AFL-CIO and 9to5, supported a United States Department of Labor lawsuit compelling Time-Warner to provide its contingent workers with normal pensions and benefits.

Politicians have heard employees' pleas for rectifying bosses' misbehavior. Patrick Buchanan, while making his bid for the Republican Party presidential nomination in 1996, condemned CEO Robert Allen and other AT&T executives for announcing 40,000 layoffs. Buchanan characterized their actions as an indicator of Corporate America's priorities in which concern for profits topped concern for workers.[39]

AT&T evidently recognized the public relations and political disaster facing it and tried hard to respond. Mr. Allen told *Newsweek* magazine how ordering cutbacks caused him personal suffering. AT&T purchased full-page advertisements in which it encouraged other organizations to hire the employees it was dismissing. And, an AT&T spokesperson explained, "If this were a prize fight of 12 rounds, I would say we lost round one; we lost round two; we fought to a draw in round three; and pretty soon we'll start winning rounds."[40]

These responses by AT&T seem to miss the message. Building and maintaining *we*, despite downsizing, is a matter of expressing intent through the introduction of genuine efforts to explore alternatives to downsizing and enhance workers' employability; it is not a matter of manipulating image. As AT&T worked on rescuing its image, its intent was apparently being read as uncaring. The company might just as well have hung out that big sign inviting *alienated workers, negative public opinion, and political intervention.*

More recently, cash balance pension plans have become a prime illustration of boss behavior that attracts government attention by alienating workers and creating a citizenry that is ripe for picking by hungry politicians. In contrast to defined benefit plans in which employees earn the bulk of their benefits during the plan's final years, benefits in cash balance plans are accrued annually, at a steady rate. Young employees might actually prefer cash balance plans because they permit more early-career job-hopping with less financial penalty. Because there is less back-loading, cash balance plans give young job-hoppers comparatively larger accumulations to carry with them to the next job.

It is when defined benefit plans are switched to cash balance plans that problems arise. This shift causes many workers serious financial harm, while simultaneously providing many companies with great financial gain. The harm occurs when a large number of veteran employees lose a great deal of future income because their employers are suddenly freed from defined benefit pension plan provisions requiring them to contribute large, latter-year benefits. The gains are realized when employers reap surpluses from pension plans that are overfunded because those large, latter-year contributions have been eliminated from the firms' future pension liabilities. In short, *their* (the employees') loss becomes *our* gain.

It is not surprising that cash balance plans have been touted by a leading benefits consulting firm as especially suited for companies "considering termination of a pension plan in order to capture overfunded assets" or those who want to reduce or modify their pension obligations.[41] Nor should anyone have been surprised in 1999, when, after protests from workers, several United States government agencies, including the Internal Revenue Service, Equal Employment Opportunity Commission, Labor Department, and General Accounting Office, began investigating the legality of cash balance plans. And, after Enron's failure, it was no surprise to learn that members of the U.S. Congress and the President were joining the pension plan debate by discussing legislation that would regulate how pension plan money could be invested, increasing the accountability of pension fund managers, and raising the likelihood of prosecution for wrongdoing.[42]

Mass media loves a target, and bosses' arrogant messages of exclusion have given them a big, fat bull's eye. If the mass media's audiences were unwilling to accept the idea that businesspeople are uncaring about their employees or society, then it would be forced to find other villains. Unfortunately for business, the idea is credible to audiences. By building we/they barriers in their organizations, bosses have also built a cadre of employees who enroll their families and friends in a group that is disillusioned with the business community. *They* do what's good for *them.*

William J. McDonough, president of the Federal Reserve Bank of New York, sounded an alarm about this growing societal danger while discussing wage disparity in the United States. *"These dramatic wage developments raise profound issues for the United States.... Issues of equity and social cohesion, issues that affect the very temperament of the country. We are forced to face the question of whether we will be able to go forward together as a unified society with a confident outlook or as a society of diverse economic groups suspicious of both the future and each other."*[43]

Third-party responses to employees' pleas, however well intended, cannot rectify the real harm created by bosses' messages of exclusion. Restrictive legislation, tax incentives for responsible behavior, and tax disincentives for irresponsible behavior are devices for engineering desired behaviors. They might compel boss behavior but, if that happens, it will occur without any increase in employees' organizational identification, because employees will easily recognize that their bosses' behaviors are attributable to compelling external pressures, not genuine intent.[44] They *don't really want to include* us, *therefore why should* we *choose to include* them?

Employee commitment cannot be legislated any more than it can be bought. No one will read coerced or instrumental boss behavior as messages of inclusion. These efforts are incapable of erecting bonds of *we* between employees and their employing organizations. They will never cause employees who are leaving their company's premises late at night to detour from a path that leads directly to the organization's front door in order to turn out the lights.

Organizations that want to strengthen employees' ties of allegiance and their motivation to advance organizational goals must curtail their most powerful privileged members' inclination to commit *we*-boosting. That can be accomplished by a consistent flow of organizational policies and procedures that affirm employees as contributors to the firm's operations, workers in the community's job market, members of groups outside of the firm that make legitimate demands (families, religious institutions and civic associations), and individuals with physical and psychological needs. Then, employees will be able to examine the three **R**s of organizational life, ask, "Am I being treated fairly, with civility, and proper recognition of my abilities?" and answer, *"Yes!"*

[1] Stewart, T. A. "See Jack. See Jack run." *Fortune* (September 27, 1999): 124–136.

[2] Useem, J. "Welcome to the new company town." *Fortune* (January 10, 2000): 62–70; "The 100 best companies to work for." *Fortune* (February 4, 2002): 72–90.

[3] Petzinger, T. Jr. "A new model for the nature of business: It's alive." *Wall Street Journal* (February 26, 1999): B1, B4.

[4] Wetlaufer, S. "Driving change: An interview with Ford Motor Company's Jacques Nasser." *Harvard Business Review* (March-April, 1999): 77–88.

[5] Wetlaufer, "Driving change: An interview with Ford Motor Company's Jacques Nasser," 79.

[6] Tichy, N. *The Leadership Engine* (New York: Harper Business, 1997).

[7] Wetlaufer, "Driving change: An interview with Ford Motor Company's Jacques Nasser," 82

[8] Tichy. *The Leadership Engine.*

[9] Bunker, B. A. and Billie T. Alban. *Large Group Interventions* (San Francisco: Jossey-Bass Publishers, 1997).

[10] Filipczak, B. "Critical mass: Putting whole systems thinking into practice." *Training* (September, 1995): 33–41.

[11] Deutsch, C. H. "The deal is done, the work begins." *New York Times* (April 11, 1999): Bu1, Bu6.

[12] Burke, W. W. and W. Trahant. *Business Climate Shifts* (Woburn, MA: Butterworth Heinemann, 2000).

13 Stewart, T. A. "See Jack. See Jack run." *Fortune* (September 27, 1999): 130.

14 Munk, N. "Organization man." *Fortune* (March 16, 1998): 62–74.

15 Lohr, S. "Though upbeat on the economy, people still fear for their jobs." *New York Times* (December 29, 1996): A1, A22.

16 "Enter Dunlap, Ax in hand." *Fortune* (December 9, 1996): 83.

17 Safire, W. "The great disconnect." *New York Times* (March 11, 1996): A17.

18 Spiers, J. "The myth of corporate greed." *Fortune* (April 15, 1996): 67–68.

19 London, M. "Redeployment and continuous learning in the 21st century: Hard lessons and positive examples from the downsizing era." *Academy of Management Executive* 10 (1996): 67–79.

20 Casio, W. F. "Guide to responsible restructuring." U.S. Department of Labor. Office of the American Workplace, 1995.

21 Rose, R. "Work Week." *Wall Street Journal* (January 30, 1996): A1.

22 Lancaster, H. "Companies promise to help employees plot their careers." *Wall Street Journal* (March 11, 1997): B1.

23 Quintanilla, C. "Work Week." *Wall Street Journal* (December 9, 1997): A1.

24 Nelson, E. *Wall Street Journal* (January 2, 1996): A1.

25 Tejadda, C. "Work Week." *Wall Street Journal* (April 2, 2002): A1.

26 Halpert, J. "The nanny is late. You have a speech. What now?" *New York Times* (April 28, 2002): Bu8.

27 Ibid.

28 Shallenbarger, S. "The secret wild card: Employees want jobs that help caregivers." *Wall Street Journal* (June 14, 2000): B1.

29 O'Brien, K. "Trends." *New York Times* (June 28, 2000): G1.

30 Quick, R. "A makeover that began at the top." *Wall Street Journal* (May 25, 2000): B1, B4.

31 Baron, R. A. "Affect and organization behavior: When and why feeling (good or bad) matters." In J. Keith Murnighan, *Social Psychology in Organizations: Advances in Theory and Research* (Englewood Cliffs, NJ: Prentice Hall, 1993).

32 Chase, M. "Weighing the benefits of mental-health days against guilt feelings." *Wall Street Journal* (September 9, 1996): B1.

33 Ibid.

34 Zachary, G. P. "The new search for meaning in 'meaningless' work." *Wall Street Journal* (January 9, 1997): B1, B2.

35 Ibid.

36 Feder, B. J. "Ministers who work among their flock." *New York Times* (October 3, 1996): D1, D20.

37 Burkins, E. "Work Week." *Wall Street Journal* (January 12, 1999): A1.

38 "Work Week." (January 25, 2000): A1.

39 Landler, M. "And now, the kinder, gentler merger." *New York Times* (April 7, 1996): E3.

40 Ibid.

41 Shultz, E. E. "Pension paternity." *Wall Street Journal* (December 28, 1999): A1, A6.

42 Chen, K. "Fight looms over pension plan changes." *Wall Street Journal* (January 22, 2002): A2; McLean, B. "Why Enron went bust." *Fortune* (December 24, 2001): 71–72; McNamee, M. and R. Miller. "How Bush would hold CEOs' feet to the fire." *Newsweek* (March 18, 2002): 58; Norris, F. "For chief, $200 million wasn't quite enough cash." *New York Times* (January 22, 2002): C1, C6.

43 Cassidy, J. "Who killed the middle class?" *The New Yorker* (October 16, 1995): 113–124.

44 Bennis, W. "A corporate fear of too much truth." *New York Times* (February 17, 2002): Wk 11.

INDEX

8 reasons why you should read the Financial Times for 4 weeks RISK-FREE!

To help you stay current with significant
developments in the world economy ...
and to assist you to make informed business
decisions — the Financial Times brings you:

❶ Fast, meaningful overviews of international affairs ... plus daily
briefings on major world news.

❷ Perceptive coverage of economic, business, financial and political
developments with special focus on emerging markets.

❸ More international business news than any other publication.

❹ Sophisticated financial analysis and commentary on world market
activity plus stock quotes from over 30 countries.

❺ Reports on international companies and a section on global investing.

❻ Specialized pages on management, marketing, advertising and
technological innovations from all parts of the world.

❼ Highly valued single-topic special reports (over 200 annually)
on countries, industries, investment opportunities, technology and more.

❽ The Saturday Weekend FT section — a globetrotter's guide to
leisure-time activities around the world: the arts, fine dining, travel,
sports and more.

The *Financial Times* delivers a world of business news.

Use the Risk-Free Trial Voucher below!

To stay ahead in today's business world you need to be well-informed on a daily basis. And not just on the national level. You need a news source that closely monitors the entire world of business, and then delivers it in a concise, quick-read format.

With the *Financial Times* you get the major stories from every region of the world. Reports found nowhere else. You get business, management, politics, economics, technology and more.

Now you can try the *Financial Times* for 4 weeks, absolutely risk free. And better yet, if you wish to continue receiving the *Financial Times* you'll get great savings off the regular subscription rate. Just use the voucher below.

Where to find tomorrow's best business and technology ideas. TODAY.

- Ideas for defining tomorrow's competitive strategies — and executing them.

- Ideas that reflect a profound understanding of today's global business realities.

- Ideas that will help you achieve unprecedented customer and enterprise value.

- Ideas that illuminate the powerful new connections between business and technology.

ONE PUBLISHER.

Financial Times Prentice Hall

FINANCIAL TIMES
Prentice Hall

WORLD BUSINESS PUBLISHER

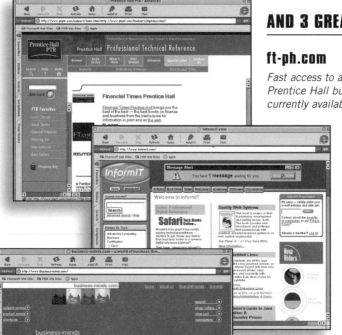

AND 3 GREAT WEB SITES:

ft-ph.com

Fast access to all Financial Times Prentice Hall business books currently available.

InformIt.com

Your link to today's top business and technology experts: new content, practical solutions, and the world's best online training.

Business-minds.com

Where the thought leaders of the business world gather to share key ideas, techniques, resources — and inspiration.